TALES
OF WILD BIRD LIFE

COCKABUNDLE ROSE AND FLEW WITH A TERRIFIC BURR OF WINGS

TALES
OF WILD BIRD LIFE

H. Mortimer Batten

Illustrated by Len Fullerton

BLACKIE: GLASGOW AND LONDON

First published 1948
This edition 1976

ISBN o 216 90276 2 (hardback)
ISBN o 216 90277 o (paperback)

Blackie and Son Limited
Bishopbriggs, Glasgow G64 2NZ
450/452 Edgware Road, London W2 1EG

Printed in Great Britain by Robert MacLehose & Co. Ltd
Printers to the University of Glasgow

CONTENTS

Tales of Wild Bird Life

HERITORS OF THE HILLS

High on the face of Cairn o' Gree, so high that a gunshot in the glen below would have reached the shelf merely in crumbling echoes, the golden eagles had their eyrie, as for many seasons past. Year after year the great pile of sticks had been renovated and added to, so that to-day the fissure in the crag face contained several cart-loads of sticks and ling, and on this seemingly precarious foundation the two down-covered eaglets were hatched. Weak-necked, pot-bellied little imps of hunger they were, and since, for many days succeeding their arrival, driving sleet and mist swept the mountain face, it took their parents all their time to nurse them through their first tender infancy. For hours the female bird

would crouch on the wind side, her wings half
spread, occasionally rising to shake the drifts of wet
snow from the folds of her feathers, and whatever
may be said of the common ruck and run of eagle
fathers, this one was an ideal father—and husband.
For it was he who fed both them and her.

In those days of bad visibility, hunting was not
easy, for even the eagles, despite their swiftness and
notorious penetration of sight, know hard times.
Not so much in winter, for when others are hungry
that is their harvest; it is during the dark days when
the mountain hares are under the peat lips and the
rabbits cosy in their crannies, that the great birds
of prey are likely to feel the pinch. That spring was,
I believe, a season of starvation for many of the birds
of prey.

One day a shepherd saw the male eagle gliding
down the corrie only fifty or sixty feet from the
ground. It was merely a flashing glimpse through
the mist wraiths, yet sufficient for the man to assure
himself that the thing which dangled from the eagle's
claws was a newly-born lamb. Thereafter, almost
daily, the shepherd missed one or more newly-born
lambs from his flock, and of course, he blamed the
eagles. He omitted to notice that, despite the weather,
he was losing no lambs in other ways, and when
eventually he solicited the aid of the stalker, that
weather-beaten son of the crags suggested to him
the common-sense line of inquiry.

"You don't need to worry your head about the
eagles, Donald," he said. " Have you ever seen an
eagle lift a living lamb? No, nor I, nor any other

shepherd or stalker I ever knew. I don't say it never happens, but I never knew it happen on this range."

The shepherd grunted, and, being a Highlander, he thought carefully before he spoke. " Well, maybe, Sandy," he admitted at length. " Maybe you're right. Possibly it's only the dead lambs they're lifting, but I won't venture an opinion till I'm sure."

Donald was never able to prove definitely that the eagles never took a living lamb, but he learnt definitely that if a lamb died, the great birds of prey would fetch it within an hour.

Sandy, the stalker, had received instructions from the proprietor of that forest not to molest the eagles, and he had no quarrel with them, but one day he witnessed a thing which altered the whole aspect. He had often noticed that the wild red deer of the hill possessed an instinctive dread of the king of birds, and he had wondered why. He had seen deer bunch together in a state of agitation immediately they caught sight of an eagle flying low, and he concluded that this instinctive dread lived on in the adult deer from the memories of their calf days, when the birds of prey might, indeed, have proved a source of danger to them. Now, however, a further explanation was presented.

Sandy noticed a small parcel of hinds running over a ridge at great speed above the mist. They were all bunched together, and their curious behaviour at once arrested his attention. Then he saw that an eagle was following them closely, and as he watched, the bird alighted on the back of one of the hinds. The terrified animal at once broke away from its companions, and started down the almost vertical descent at breakneck speed. Evidently it was blind with terror, for next moment it threw itself headlong over a low cliff, to crash with a broken thigh among the boulders some distance below. As it fell, the eagle let go its hold, and went wheeling round, presently to close its wings, and drop where the luckless hind had dropped.

Was this, indeed, what the bird of prey had aimed at? Sandy had no doubt, and forthwith he hurried to an adjacent croft and obtained the loan of a shotgun. With the mist in his favour he stalked to the edge of the cliff, and there, sure enough, was the eagle, standing on the dead deer.

Five minutes later Sandy stood, the wet mist driving down his swarthy face, looking at the great bird, which lay outstretched at his feet. He spread one of the great wings. " The hen bird!" he thought, having in mind the eyrie on Cairn o' Gree. " She must have been half starved, and she looks it."

That, indeed, was the first time the female eagle had left her chicks since they were hatched, driven from them, at length, by her need, and so she paid the price of hunger, which is the common coin of death in the wilderness. But she had established a sad precedent, for the tale lost nothing as it sped from range to range, and stalkers who, hitherto, had never raised a hand against the royal birds, now regarded with suspicion the wildness of their hinds. But, had that spring been a normal spring, there would have been no Cairn o' Gree incident, to be quoted against the eagles as an accepted habit of the kind—no conclusive proof that the mighty hunter of the air is a menace admittedly to red deer calves and lambs, for its destruction of adult deer was proven.

As a matter of fact, there was no creature in that range the eagles had need to fear, excepting man, of course, and man they feared because he no longer stands as Nature made him. He has gained unequal power by reason of shot and powder, and even man the Cairn o' Gree eagles feared little. One day, for example, a visiting sportsman was fishing the arm of the loch, which runs far inland through the range, where a mountain torrent pours down over the crags into the brackish waters—fishing, I say, but in truth he was paying less attention to his sport than to the wonderful sunlight and cloud effects which surrounded him. Away to the west a burst of sunshine played on the snow-capped heights, and through the fissures of the clouds, rolling low above a choppy sea, the ladders of heaven streamed fantastically. Though midday, the fireplay was darkly wonderful, and now and then a sea trout would leap from the blue, glistening like a bar of silver, to plunge and ricochet across the surface in a radiant display of energy.

Suddenly the angler heard a swish overhead, and in the fantastic light he saw what might have been a streak of golden fire descending. It struck the surface only forty feet from him, casting high a cloud of sparkling spray, and it was only later that he realized just what he had seen. He had seen a silver trout shoot up from the deep, but ere it broke the surface, he heard the swish of wings above. Evidently the eagle had been watching, and he was midway down in his stoop ere the trout appeared. So he caught that silver, glistening bar in mid-leap —snatched it three feet from the surface in a mile-eating, headlong plunge. The angler himself was never to forget what he had seen, for as an example of stunt flying it was incredible, and as the eagle rose from the loch, at first flapping heavily ere it got into its glide, the bar of silver hung limply from its claws.

Thus the male eagle, feeding his chicks, alone and unaided, had, indeed, to turn his hand to many trades. He himself could feed on almost anything, carrion included, but he preferred the freshly killed for his chicks. Even had his mate lived, his responsibilities would have been heavy enough, but now it was he who had to shield them from the storms which would have frozen them rigid in the eyrie, besides finding food for them and himself.

The angler who had seen the trout incident was an occasional contributor to the sporting press— that is, he wrote when he had anything special to write about, and one of his subsequent articles was headed—" Do Eagles Hunt by Night?". He knew nothing about the killing of the hen eagle, and so his opening passage read—" I have reason to believe they do. I was passing by the hill road from the loch, past the foot of Cairn o' Gree, to the hotel, at 10.45 p.m. It was quite clear and moonlight, though all day, as for several preceding days, a driving mist had shut everything from view. Suddenly I heard a loud swish overhead—a sound which I recognized instantly as the descent of an eagle, half stooping, half gliding. Looking up, I saw what might have been a human garment borne by the wind. It passed over, sweeping in a bee line for some wet and glistening crags on the slope eighty yards away. There I lost sight of it, but I heard instantly the piercing scream of a mountain hare, and a second or two later the ' zipp-zipp-zipp ' of an eagle's wings as it rose. This was three hours after sunset, and as I have intimated, the visibility by the light of the moon was a great deal better than it had been through the day."

So we have good reason to think that the widower eagle put in no little overtime to meet his growing demands, but all the same, the male chick perished. Sandy found it lying pulped at the foot of the crags —fallen from the eyrie, no doubt, though there was quite a likely chance that the hen chick, feeling the pinch of short rations, had kicked it out.[1]

At length fair weather came, and Sandy, who lived across the glen from Cairn o' Gree, remarked to his wife: " You watch now it's turned clear! I bet that eagle brings another mate along to help him feed the chicks."

But Sandy's wife had other things to do than watch eagles, and her circumstances in life did not encourage betting. Anyway, she told Sandy that mates were not so easy to find as his experience had

---

[1] The chicks of the golden eagle are always cock and hen, the female being the larger.

led him to think, to which Sandy good-naturedly retorted, after due thought: "If he's got any sense he'll remain a bachelor and boss his own roost!"

Indeed the eagle did remain " a bachelor ", for his kind was not exactly superfluous even in that remote range, though the distances he covered were enormous. He seemed to have regular beats, for every four days or so the stalker in the Glen o' Weeping saw an eagle (which was not one of his native Black Mount eagles) systematically working down a certain corrie. That was fourteen miles from Cairn o' Gree, and again a keeper on the slopes of Ben Lawers saw a solitary bird working those slopes—forty-six miles from Cairn o' Gree. Again, when the north wind blew, this same wanderer might have been seen over the shores of Loch Awe, and even as far as Loch Lomond—wheeling and soaring over the flights of gulls, higher than the topmost gull, higher even than the buzzards which soared above the gulls.

Yet, for all the distance, he, the King of Birds, was unmistakable—not only by the gliding majesty of his flight, which the great black-backed gulls closely rivalled, but by the golden sheen as he turned in the light, by the occasional narrowness of his circles, above all, by the upward tilt of his wing tips.

When Sandy heard the fisherman's story about the catching of the sea trout, he shook his head incredulously, and said: "Not the Cairn o' Gree eagles! Maybe a sea eagle from one of the islands, but I never heard of a black [1] eagle taking fish."

[1] Golden.

" No?" replied the stranger indifferently. " And until a fortnight ago, Sandy, no one would have convinced you that a golden eagle will attack deer. Anyway, it was worth seeing."

Sandy did not argue the point, but a little further on he said: " If you want to see some real flying, keep your eyes on Cairn o' Gree any fine evening now. The old bird will be coaxing the chick to leave the nest."

So it was, indeed, that the male eagle, having very faithfully and ably fulfilled his duties single-handed, now began to think of launching his charge upon the infinite world. Alone he had fed his offspring, shielded it from storms, and fulfilled those duties which his mate should have shouldered with him, and now, one cloudless evening, he hung in the wind opposite the eyrie. He hung motionless, his great planes set at an angle to the wind, and a listener in the glen might have heard for the first time the call note of the great birds of prey. So habitually silent were they that, from the day when the first new twig was laid until to-day, when the sole surviving chick had left the eyrie and was ready to fly, no call notes had been uttered. Few indeed are those who have heard the voice of a golden eagle, as it might have been heard that evening had there been anyone to hear—a thin, faint " Kee ". For fully a minute he hung, then slightly altering the angle of his planes, he rose, up, up, into the dazzling light, till even Cairn o' Gree was flattened out in the level map of sea and loch and range. He could follow mighty rivers from their sources to the sea, and such human habitations as there were showed as the merest specks scattered as from an " empty " pepper pot.

Then in mid-heaven the eagle closed his wings, and like a blob of molten gold he fell, to swish past the eyrie where his daughter was watching, then to curve and sweep and glide. And his daughter at length spread her wide wings, which were her fortune, and boldly launched herself upon the world.

A few days later the two eagles parted, but one would have thought that by the ordinary course it was for the chick to go forth into the world to find her own range. Was it that the father said to her: " My child—undividedly my own—this is my range by right of heritage, and by that right I leave it now to you. It is the way of the eagles to mate for life, and here in the ancestral eyrie where you yourself were reared, may you rear your offspring—many of them. Your father is growing old, but not so old that he wishes to remain alone. Therefore he is going to explore new hills, and maybe he will not return. And so—farewell! If you can't be good, my child, at any rate be happy."

There are some who say that the eagle cannot die by the hand of time alone. Many years are given him, but when his hour comes, age alone cannot strike the blow. Tradition tells us that he flies away to sea, following the sunset, even as the shadows close on his native range; some believe that his own kind beat him down, or that man or his wild foes must strike the inevitable blow. Time unaided cannot sound the final call, and this much would seem true—that when his springs are numbered, there comes to the royal bird a desire to explore new lands, and so he leaves his native range. Perhaps that explains the old, old story that the eagle dies at sea.

One day that autumn, a keeper in the Hampshire coverts was much mystified by the strange conduct of his pheasants. In the woods all round they were flying from point to point, and crowing on the fence tops, and as the man emerged into the beech avenue, he saw an immense bird sweeping over the tree tops. Though he had never seen the like of it before, he knew it to be a bird of prey, and the cause of the pheasants' unrest. From force of habit he threw up his gun, firing both barrels in quick succession. He saw the feathers fly, but the eagle wheeled and rose, up and up till the merest speck in the heavens, then gliding easily, it turned towards the north.

Next day Sandy was on the hill when again he saw two eagles over the heights of Cairn o' Gree. So he concluded that the bird he had seen alone for several days had obtained a mate, for they were circling together in closest company. Then, as he watched, one of the two staggered in its flight and began to descend. Sandy thought at first that it was stooping at some living speck in the glen below, but as it fell, the great wings opened and it began to spin. So headlong down, flashing as the sunbeams caught it, it struck the ground not far from where the stalker stood.

Sandy went over, and stood looking down at the dead creature. " Old age, I reckon," was his summing up, for he saw that the eagle was very, very old; then he remembered that a wild free eagle

cannot die by time alone. He raised one of the outspread wings, and on the crumpled feathers of the
breast he saw a crimson stain. This, then, explained
it, and as he stood there wondering, he heard aloft a
sound which he had never heard before—the thin-
edged " kee " of a golden eagle.

THE POOL OF BLOSSOMS

At the foot of the old Manse garden, the stream widened out under the corner chestnut tree, and formed quite a spacious pool—at this season a very beautiful pool, for the chestnut was in heavy blossom, and among the branches fell a spray of laburnum, crowding shoulder to shoulder with the crab-apple tree. It was a corner of blossoms; blossoms floated on the surface of the pool, intermingled with the foam flakes; blossoms overhead, and blossoms and their petals underfoot. The air was full of their sweet fragrance, and intermingling with the scent sounded the lively chipp of the chaffinches and the song of the garden warblers.

A French naturalist once said that in England there is a chaffinch for every branch, but in that tiny corner of Scotland there was not only a chaffinch for every branch, but there was a chaffinch for every tiny pebble which rose above the bubble and swirl. Even then there were chaffinches left over for the sandy margins—a modest and unobtrusive company, save for their occasional bursts of song and for the flashes of white wing bars which betrayed their numbers to the keen observer. In truth, they were almost as numerous as the flowers, for this was one of those hidden-away little corners which no man seemed ever to have discovered—or at least, only one man! The chaffinches sang, the sunlight fell on

swinging flakes, the blossoms filled the air with light
and scent, the musical murmur of the shallows above
and below was part of the general harmony.

There came a flutter of wings, and on the narrow
sandy margin, where the shadows of the chestnut
fell, a visitor alighted. He, too, was in keeping with
the scene, almost a fairy spirit of the place, for it was
a fantail pigeon from the Manse dovecote. He
alighted at the water's edge, I say, and about his
pink feet were the toe marks and the claw marks of
other pigeons, indicating that this was their recognized drinking-place; and as he pouted and paused,
he might have been a flower shed from the overhanging trees. Obviously he had come to drink, for
though it was cool down there at the water's edge,
the outer world was simmering with heat.

But the fantail did not drink. Though tame to
the border of stupidity, he seemed to be ill at ease
and uncertain of his ground. Twice he went to the
water's edge, and twice he withdrew. He tried a
third time, but drew back quickly, as though afraid
of his own reflection as he dipped his head. What
on earth ailed him? Why was he afraid of the water?
One could not have told, but afraid of it he certainly
was, and finally he rose with a double clap of wings,
and disappeared among the blossoms. It was just
as though some unseen guardian of the Wild Folk
had whispered a warning to him, and he was gone.

But the drinking-place was not for long to remain
deserted, for there came another flurry of wings, and
down through the green leaves descended two black
forms, chipping each other as they came—the un-

mistakable jackdaw call. One of them alighted by
the water, the other on a briar spray above, and as
they alighted, the chaffinches scattered from point
to point, for the jackdaws are not to be trusted.
Obviously they, too, had come to drink, yet they did
not drink. They remained only ten seconds, for the
one at the water hopped back to his mate on the
spray, which would not bear them both, so as it
yielded both flew off with a call of complaint—to
drink elsewhere. And the chaffinches rallied back to
repossess the little gravel margin, their numbers
supplemented now by a pair of yellow wagtails
which darted and waggled and stood awhile—
melancholy little figures, contemplating their reflections in the mirror where they stood.

Yet soon another came, a wood pigeon from the
larch woods, to alight with an elegant swish headlong through the blossoms, and one knew not of his
coming till he was there. Strange to say, the chaffinches made no stir for him; evidently they knew
from the sound of his wings that he was just a peaceful cushie doo, and on the whole, I think he was
more lovely than the fantail, this wild thing from
the hillsides, alive with furtive watchfulness, and
very much awake. Perfectly groomed he was, and perfectly attired, and his bright eyes instantly took in
everything. He craned his neck and listened, then,
pink and blue and grey, he strutted proudly and con-
fidently to the crystal edge of the drinking-place.

But he did not drink. One moment he was there,
and the next there was just a clap of wings, and he
had departed like a ray of light. Strange that!

CONTEMPLATING THEIR REFLECTIONS

What was there about the pool to-day? Nothing one could see. Here a dragon-fly darted and hovered, there a moth fluttered, or a daddy-long-legs trailed perilously among the foam flakes. Not even a trout rose—the surface was a mirror, save for the flowers and the idle flakes. The water, too, was as clear as crystal; one could see every pebble and every stone save where it sank to deepest green towards the depths at its centre, yet the birds would not drink to-day—that is, the larger birds, though the chaffinches and the wagtails and the lesser folk were all at home.

For ten minutes nothing special happened, and the thing that happened next—well, it just happened. There was no introduction, no swish of wings or rumble of paws or cracking of twigs. It simply happened, and that was the beginning and the end of it.

Just a zipp and a slash and a splash, and the chaffinches scattering like chaff in a gale. They rose for the branches, they flew upstream and down and to left and right. It was as though a thunderbolt had fallen, and there, indeed, the thunderbolt was, at the water's edge—a sparrow hawk, and pinned under his claws, pinned into the wet sand and partly awash, was a crumpled little heap of feathers which had been a chaffinch.

The claw-like beak of the bird of prey was ready to strike should its victim flutter, but there was no need to deal that blow. He had pounded it into the sand, crushed the life out of it in one vicious grab, so he stood there, his bright eyes peering round, perfectly still save for the flash of his eyes. He, too, made a picture, but a very different picture, that fierce, defiant killer of the air, afraid of nothing save man. And man played no part in this scene. He looked savagely exalted over his kill, yet he was in no hurry this season of plenty. He stood at the water's edge and, because it was hot, he lowered his head to drink, and again something happened— rather something *had* happened. Something rose from the depths of the pool, but one did not see its rise. From the depths of the pool it must have come, but there was just a cloud of spray, a surge of white bubbles, a savage scream, a lunge, and the rings spreading and widening, the lap-lap of water about the narrow sandy shore, and about the exit doors of the water voles. The sparrow hawk was gone, leaving only that one stab of sound to mark his going, leaving only a trail of feathers among the foam flakes to mark the place from which he had been snatched from life, and no sooner was he gone than the chaffinches came back by unseen ways, till soon there was a chaffinch for every branch and a chaffinch for every pebble.

Just then the old minister came sauntering down with his short, stiff rod, his enormous float and bait can, to fish for the pike which lived in the pool. That pike had afforded him three years of steady fishing, but perhaps the minister would triumph in the end. Yet had you told him that ten minutes ago the proper bait would have been a living sparrow hawk, or perhaps a cushie doo, would he have believed it?

CHILDREN OF THE MIST

High on the face of Meall nan Tarmachan, higher even than the heather grows, the mother ptarmigan hatched her chicks. So small were they when they left the richly-marbled shells, that the family of nine might have been comfortably housed in a fair-sized breakfast cup, yet no sooner had the last of them shaken off its fetters, than their vagabond lives began, and they left the nest for all time.

The visitor to that aloof and rugged region would have been appalled by the utter loneliness of it. Here and there grey cloud banks drifted, blotting everything from view. There was never a sound about the broken wash-outs other than the moaning of the wind. At times a white hare might have started from one's feet. Here and there one might have seen the tracks of deer about the peat bogs, now and then one might have heard the rattling croak of the ptarmigan; but all save the hares were invisible, and even they were ghosts in their ghostly setting.

Why, then, was the mother ptarmigan so deadly afraid? The deer would not harm her, nor yet the hares, but she kept the tiny chicks under her half-raised wings as she led them away, and ever her keen eyes scanned the mountain face. Very slowly she moved, pecking at the earth, " clucking " to the chicks to encourage them to search for food; and so by gentle stages they gained at length a trickling stream at which she drank, the chicks imitating her, spluttering and choking a good deal, but no doubt getting down the water they needed.

Suddenly there sounded a soft, frog-like croak from somewhere up the slope, and instantly the mother flattened, the chicks under her, her neck rigidly outstretched against the ground. A moment ago she had been just a brown mottled bird on the stony earth, but now she ceased to be. She became one of the thousand thousand stones about her, and not even a chameleon could have camouflaged itself so wonderfully. There might have been eyes on earth which could pick her out, but not human eyes, and certainly clumsy human feet would have trodden her under.

There was a burr of wings, and another ptarmigan, hitherto unseen, rose with a second warning croak from the slope fifty feet higher up. He flashed overhead, pitching and swerving, and there came from the direction in which he was flying something which looked like a sheet of brown paper, borne on the wind. It wheeled, circling idly, fifty or sixty feet above the ground—clearly a bird of prey, and in the uncertain light it looked the size of an eagle.

But the mother ptarmigan knew that it was no eagle, and so did her mate. Had it been, he would not have dared to show himself thus, flying boldly to meet it, thereby diverting attention from his family. In normal times neither he nor his wife had any fear of the buzzard, but their fear now was for their chicks, and so the mother ptarmigan remained absolutely still, while the hunter of the air wheeled and wafted and pirouetted out of sight.

Such passing thrills were to be of almost hourly occurrence in the lives of the ptarmigan family, but not always did the mother gather her chicks under her, and trust so implicity to her protective colouring. The little chicks were growing with the hours, and in vitality they grew even more rapidly than in bulk. So by evening on the second day they were dodging among the Alpine plants, the bolder spirits fully a yard away from mother, when again that warning croak sounded up the slope, followed as before by the strong burr of wings.

The mother ptarmigan must have known in some mysterious way what was coming, for this time she acted very differently. She rose as her mate had risen and went burring off, leaving the chicks to take their chances, and as she left them, each minute atom of grousehood crouched and flattened just as she had flattened yesterday.

Such desertion seemed callous on the mother's part, but the reason for it became clear when a minute or so later a lean, grey-stockinged mountain fox came trotting down the slope, sifting every gust with his keen nostrils. He paused within ten paces of the ptarmigan chicks, and from the keen alertness of his amber eyes one would have thought that nothing would escape him, yet he saw them not, though had their mother been crouching there he would both have seen and smelt her. So her presence would merely have betrayed her helpless brood.

On the third day of their lives the ptarmigan

chicks were to see one of the rarest and certainly the strangest and most wonderful creature of their lives. Slow it was of movement, for it came toiling up the rugged hillside with heavy breath and clumsy, straggling feet. The mother ptarmigan knew of its coming long before it came, for as before her mate had warned her, though this time he did not rise in flight. A wonderful father he was, seeming to play no part in the lives of his chicks, yet in point of fact he it was who faced every peril for them.

So the heavy-footed creature came shuffling up the slope, and strange to say, the mother ptarmigan feared him no more than she would have feared an approaching deer or hare. She did not shepherd her chicks under her, nor did she fly away, and next moment the man, for such it was, saw her and her family running along the barren earth almost at his feet. The mother was all puffed out, and looked as though for two peas she would turn back and show fight, but the man stopped dead for fear of stepping upon a chick which might have chosen to crouch. He saw that at the tail end of the procession was a chick which had difficulty in getting over the earth, for it was weak on its legs, so this man, who knew well the wild folk of the hill, did what seemed a ruthless thing. He raised a heavily nailed hill boot, and crushed the lame chick under it, and the mother never knew of her loss.

Why did the stalker choose to do this? Because he knew that the lame chick would handicap the rest, holding them back in the eternal struggle to keep abreast with their food requirements, and that, thus handicapped, others might become lame, and all would have suffered.

So one lame chick may lead to the loss of the whole brood, and in any case the stalker knew that the crippled atom of life would very soon fall and perish. There is no place for the unfit at that altitude.

There was little incident in the lives of the young ptarmigan at this period, save the constant passing of their foes. Now and then an eagle was seen, far and aloft, but always the mother would creep into the nearest thicket, remaining hidden till the peril was past.

One morning—it was the sixth day, and the chicks were now as quick as mice—father uttered the usual warning, and as before mother rose and flew straight off. Then there came down the hillside, darting from cranny to cranny, at times making the most astounding leaps from shelf to shelf, a creature un-like any other creature they had seen. Part ermine he was, for, like the ermine of the drifts, he sought the shadowy crannies, but he was larger than the ermine, and in his floating mode of progress there was something which suggested a creature of the trees. Over and above this, he possessed a canary yellow waistcoat, which was his *sine qua non*, and a bushy tail which he used as a rudder.

In truth the newcomer belonged to a very ancient race, whose pedigree as a creature of man's hearth is older than that of *felis caffra*; he was a true blue-blooded aristocrat of the hills, which, however, did not improve matters from the point of view of the ptarmigan chicks. This was a past master in the

3

savage art of hunting, and for days past he had amused himself hunting ptarmigan chicks. Indeed, he had nothing to learn in that superfine art.

So he found the crouching brood, and one by one he slew them. There was just a snarl and a squeak, and a ptarmigan chick was gone. He had killed five when the father and mother came back. They came skimming the barren earth, and they alighted claws first at break-neck speed, and their claws were presented to the marten.

The female was the first to land, but swift and silent though she was the killer saw her coming. He leapt to meet her, and they met in mid-air, with just a thud and a cloud of feathers. The marten was carried backwards, and they fell six feet apart—fell and bounced and ricochetted, and thereafter the mother ptarmigan did not stir.

But her mate, wheeling, dashed in, his feathered, owl-like feet presented to the foe. His claws closed upon the killer's face ere that live wire could recover from its fall, and there followed a hissing shriek, then the cock ptarmigan was tossed aside. He was up in an instant, as indeed he had need to be, for there followed the click and the parry and again the rattle of wings.

The cock ptarmigan did his best, but above their defensive instincts wild parents are mercifully endowed with the knowledge that if they sell their lives the end for which they fight is lost. Fear they know not when defending their young, but a small voice whispers: " If you die, then those for whom you fight will also die!"

THE MARTEN WAS CARRIED BACKWARDS

So when at length the aristocrat with the yellow waistcoat went his murderous way, there remained only two chicks living—one which had wriggled into a mouse hole, and another which had wriggled after it.

An hour later the male ptarmigan started off down the mountain face, followed by the two distinguished survivors. He had looked at the dead thing which was once his mate, but he had not seemed to recognize her, for still he called and searched elsewhere. He had called for his chicks after looking at their little trampled corpses, and when at sundown only the two at his side peeped reassuringly for the rest, craning their necks to see above the pebbles, he swallowed his loss and set off to face the future.

Down the rugged slope he led, but the chicks were tired, and every time he paused they nestled under his feathers with sleepy peeps, but there was no rest in his soul. Still down he led them; at times they fell off boulders, at times one or other found itself unable to scale some obstacle, and peeped most desperately. But father, because he was father, bore remorselessly on.

It was night now, though almost as light as day, and the ghostly world of the mountain heights had become peopled with ghosts. Whence came all the mountain hares? The very earth was covered with them, and everywhere could be heard the thumping of their strong hind paws. There sounded, too, the whistling of dotterel, of golden plovers and redshanks, and the siren-like pipings of the curlews lower down. There came the crowing of red grouse.

and somewhere in the infinite a snipe was drumming as he wheeled in prodigious circles. Overhead was the burr and rattle of the ptarmigan thousands, those mysterious folk which, mysterious in themselves, are even more so because they belong to a land whose laws no man can understand. It was one of those still nights of early spring when every sound carries and every creature is astir.

At midnight the father ptarmigan and his chicks gained the edge of the heather line—a peat ridge covered with straggling ling. Here, in the deep shelter, father settled himself, puffing out his feathers as mother had done, and long after his two little charges were sound asleep, he kept on clucking and tucking still more imaginary chicks under his wings. For he was, as we have said, a good father.

By the ordinary course of nature it was for the male ptarmigan to mount to some high point and to watch for his family, but misfortune had thrust upon him duties of an entirely different kind, and very nobly he rose to them. He must, indeed, have reasoned out that his mate was dead, and that therefore he must shoulder her duties.

But his responsibilities were short-lived, for on the seventh day the two chicks, no larger than sparrows, had acquired their flight feathers, and were able to take short, swift flights after their father. This opened up a new phase of their lives, for the difficulty of getting from place to place was now removed. The ptarmigan, the children of the barren heights, use their wings much more than do the grouse of the lower slopes. The food of the

grouse is on every side, and so their daily requirements do not demand long flights. Later on, when
the sun became hot, the grouse would fly down to
the shady bracken slopes for the heat of the day, and
back towards evening, but the ptarmigan need their
wings every day and at all seasons, since their food
is sparingly scattered over a great area.

Every day now was crammed with incident, and
so, too, were the nights. There was little darkness in
the north country at this season, and when, for
example, an eagle flew overhead at noon, the ptarmigan would hide, and for many hours they would
remain secretive. Then, after sundown, they would
creep forth to feed. Here and there would sound
the " croak-croak-croak ", and here and there the
whirling rattle, and in the wan, unearthly light, grey
at those altitudes, but deepening into purple on the
lower slopes, the hillside would become peopled
with strange little folk, haunting the stream edge
where the tundra ended and the moor began. Overhead the air was dark with ptarmigan, coming and
going, and soon they dotted all the earth, swarming
about the creeping plants, picking up morsels of
sprouting greenery hidden among the stones and
pebbles.

So for an hour or more this place would be alive
with them, then suddenly, mysteriously, without
sound, the birds of the mists would go as though the
very mists had swallowed them.

But a minute or two later another scene would
change. High among the phosphorescent clouds,
trailing their muslin mantles across the rocky face—in

a deep, dim corrie where the stag-moss creeps, and where the cloudberry cowers from the upland blast —something would happen. To-night, save for the radiant cloud wraiths, the air was sparkingly, radiantly clear. One could see every hair on the fronds of the stag-moss, every sparkling jewel on the face of the granite, but not a thing stirred as yet—not a sound was audible.

Then the ptarmigan would come. Like a clap of the hand the ground would become creeping with them. Ptarmigan, ptarmigan everywhere, swarming like ants about a pine hill, while the air above vibrated with their wings. Yet the birds themselves were invisible, and it was only their shadows one saw.

It was a wonderful world to which these creatures belonged, especially when the moon was bright. Fantastic cloud formations stretched below, upon a sea of pearl-white strata, ridged and billowed, stretching on through the infinite mystery of the heavens, and through the black rifts lay the earth of glen and strath, dotted like a draughtboard, with its green pastures and steadings, and its squares of fallow and forest, and the silver Dochart winding in and out to where Loch Tay stretched like a sheet of burnished platinum. Then the clouds would shift and silt and split asunder, and behold!—behold the mighty landscape, filled with unending promise! Scenes so unreal, so far removed from the ordinary aspects of life, that no pen can describe them.

Or again there was nothing save the moon and the stars and the silver lining of the clouds below, and all around the black ridges, towering upwards, then dark shapes would come and go without sound, without even the click of cloven hoofs in that eternal world of drifting ghosts. No wonder that the ptarmigan were strange birds, living amid such strange settings, which were for ever demonstrating some new trick on the part of the goddess from whose sieve the raindrops fall.

Once we saw how the Alpine hares gather on the moonlit heights, to leap and chase each other and to run in aimless circles, and so also at times do the Alpine ptarmigan foregather at certain places. It was not food which drew them, nor yet the desire to mate and marry, and it might be day-time or night-time when they met at certain places which they have frequented for these strange orgies for ages past. Train after train, and pack after pack, the birds of the mist would come streaming in to perch upon the boulders, to strut about in the open, the hens and their chicks croaking and calling, the male birds scraping their wings and performing like heathens at a feast. For thirty minutes or more these strange meetings would last, then with rising, dipping flight, still calling as they flew, the packs would split apart, and silence would close again on the rugged scene.

So spring merged into summer, and when the big stags descended with their antlers clean, there came the rattle of guns and the bark of the stalker's rifle. The grouse paid their heavy toll, but to the ptarmigan of the greater heights it meant little. It has been said that there is but one greater fool than the ptarmigan, which never really learns the fear of man, and that the man who climbs for them. Not that these birds of the tundra afford poor sport, for their flight is dazzlingly swift, and amidst their broken surroundings they come and go in the twinkling of an eye, but between the heather where the grouse butts stand and the stony heights of the ptarmigan, there is a wide gulf fixed. And so, secure in their castle of the skies, the grey birds listened to the rattle of death below, but for them the days succeeding the twelfth brought no horrors.

One evening there sounded the vicious bark of a rifle, echoing and re-echoing through the long defiles, and a little while later a mighty stag came plunging up the hillside into ptarmigan land. His head hung low, his great flanks heaved, his tongue hung from his saliva-covered jaws, but wearily, frenziedly, with many a slip of his splayed hoofs, he made his way upwards, while an old hind ran round him, watching him frightened-eyed. Once he paused and looked defiantly back across the emptiness below, and as he paused he staggered and began to slide. Desperately he strove to recover himself, but the moving stones gave way beneath him, and down he fell, giddily down, rolling, spinning, crashing from shelf to shelf, while there sounded the thud and the hack of ivory on rock. And from the heights above a hundred pairs of ptarmigan eyes watched and wondered, and a hundred ptarmigan voices croaked their vague dismay at this tragedy of the heights.

When autumn came to the valley, winter came to

the heights. Each night brought its bitter frosts, and the trickle and ooze from the shelves formed into giant beards of ice. At midday the sun was still hot, and the ptarmigan went in packs down to the lower levels to drink at the moss pools, but for the most part the dawning of winter made them even more truly Alpine than before.

Now when the cold winds blew, the father ptarmigan and his two chicks flew to the greatest height of all, where the best shelter they knew awaited them. For here there was a great fissure which was never clear of snow, and when, through their glasses, the stalkers saw the ptarmigan heading for this drift at sundown, they knew that the night was to bring wild weather.

Had one examined the drift one would have found its surface perforated with the roosting holes of the Alpine birds. Rising high above the drift they would dive head foremost into it, breaking through the frozen crust, then they would squirm and burrow till deeply hidden. Thus the whole glacier was honeycombed, and there, secure from storm and frost, they roosted.

One day—and the leaves in the valley were drifting now—there occurred a greater congress of these strange folk than we have ever seen before. They met in a lonely wind-swept place, where stood a cairn of stones—all the ptarmigan from all the slopes, the males to strut in the open, scraping their wings defiantly, while the hen birds and the chicks of the season craned their necks and added at least the support of their voices to the ceremony. I doubt whether five per cent knew why they were there or what it was all about, yet more came and ever more, for this evidently was a mighty ptarmigan ceremony. Some had attained their full white dress, and were invisible save for their shadows and their black tail feathers, but the majority of the gathering were patched and mottled midway between the brown of summer and the white of the snows.

Why had they forgathered thus at this place and at this season? Why all this confusion and this many-voiced complaint? It was not one of their customary meeting-places, yet here they were, old and young, as though forgathered to settle some event on which their race depended. Why?

There, under the cairn of stones, lay a very ancient foe, old as the eagle. Very low he crouched amidst his icy settings, as though ashamed of the ignominy of his plight—as though, indeed, to hide his aristo-cratic canary-yellow waistcoat. He looked at the ptarmigan with eyes which were living jewels, but there was no light of battle in those eyes, nor yet the light of fear and defeat, for it is not the way of his kind to know when they are down. Yet a helpless captive he lay, held down by a frozen stone which his rest-less paws had moved, and which was frozen hard to the frozen ground.

JEFF'S PET

When the incident occurred, Jeff Anderson was fishing at the foot of the long line of rapid water just where it joins the deep under the shadows of Bennoir Wood. The sun was low in the west, and there was a considerable glare and glitter on the surface, which the wreaths of rising spray enhanced, so that even eyes so keenly trained as Jeff's had some difficulty in seeing what was coming, and he did not see the bird at all till it actually struck his rod. He was just in the act of casting, and the impact was so violent that the rod was thrown from his hand. He snatched it up before it could drift away, noticing that the bird, whatever it was, had fallen stunned into the water, and was whirling rapidly downstream; so, prompted mainly by curiosity, he hurried down and fished it out in his landing-net. It was a young long-eared owl, just independent of its parents.

Jeff thought at first that it was dying, for it merely gasped weakly, and he saw that one of its wings was broken; but he was not a believer in the convenient principle of putting things out of their misery. Like most skilled anglers, he was clever with his fingers, and also a bit of a vet, so he took out his fly-tying kit and soon had the wing firmly in splints. He put the dying bird in his creel and by the time he reached home it was very much alive, its injured wing tied down to its side. Five minutes later it was perched on his arm, ravenously devouring bits of raw meat.

Evidently that young owl had a good deal to learn, for it knew nothing of the fear of man. Jeff took it into the old barn, which was an owl's paradise of shady nooks, rafters, hay-seeds, and cobwebs, and when he went in to do the milking next morning, it was perched on a cow stall, and came to him instantly when he held out some food. Though it could not fly, it was capable of the most surprising jumps, assisted by its sound wing, and it was not very long before the owl found its way to the big cross beam fifteen feet from the ground. There in the dense shadows it would perch all day, but as soon as the cows came home it would descend to be fed.

Jeff's ginger cat paid no attention to the newcomer, nor it to him, and soon even the cows came to regard the bird as part of the furnishings, for while Jeff milked, it would perch on the back of the cow he was milking, and so from cow to cow, wheezing and moaning an unmusical accompaniment to the swish-swish-swish of the milk. But as the days passed, the necessity of feeding it with meat ceased, for the barn was full or rats and mice, and so Jeff's pet began to pay its way. Any morning one might have witnessed the unique spectacle of an owl drinking milk from a saucer, for the bird had acquired the habit of sharing the daily ration with the cat.

It is not very often that a creature which belongs by birth and long heritage to the Wild acquires any real affection for man. It may come to his call and even fawn against the hand which feeds it, but food and expectation are the ruling motives. So highly

THAT YOUNG OWL HAD A GOOD DEAL TO LEARN

intelligent a beast as a fox may show every sign of affection for the man who has reared it, but its love for him is only skin-deep. Almost in a day it will forget him, and when next his hand is extended towards it, it may respond with a dagger's thrust. So much is true of even the highest wild beasts, the fox, the otter, the hand-reared deer, and generally speaking, wild birds are far below them, except perhaps the corvines, and an owl is not a corvine. He is just a feathered cat of the night, as wild as any wild cat of the corries, and therefore it was doubly strange that even after it no longer looked to Jeff for food, this owl sought his company.

In the dusk of an evening, when the man went out into the orchard-scented air, it would hobble across the yard at his heels, looking like some strange hunch-backed little dwarf, and from this it was but one step to finding its way to the kitchen. Ere long, while Jeff smoked his pipe beside the big stone kitchen hearth, his cat under his chair, his sheep dog at his feet, this strange newcomer was added to the group, seated by his shoulder on the high back of the old oak chair. It treated Mrs. Jeff with cold indifference, and for a long time it could not tolerate strangers.

It was owing to this latter shyness that Jeff learnt that the hearing of an owl must be marvellously keen, for all at once the bird would leave his chair and hop through the window and away over to the barn, or if the window were closed, it would mount to an oak rafter and take hiding in a favourite corner of the ceiling. Three minutes later the dog would get up and bark, and yet another minute and they would hear a visitor's footfall on the cobbled walk outside. This order of things was invariable, and Jeff concluded that the owl could actually hear the click of the gate on the occupation road as the visitor left the highway, though the gate was fully half a mile away, with trees and a stream between.

" People talk about the silent flight of the owl so that its quarry cannot hear it," Jeff remarked to a fisherman friend, " but I've always thought that the silent flight is so that the owl can hear its quarry. Watch an owl quartering the ground, and you will see he hunts by sound as much as by sight. I've always thought so, and I'm sure of it now."

" Maybe you're right," replied the other lover of the gentle art. " Anyway, you won't keep owls out of a barn containing rats and mice, even if you want to, which isn't likely. They'll come from far and near to a rat-infested building, and how do they know what is inside except by hearing?"

By now the injured wing was healed, so Jeff took off the wrappings. He did not really want to lose his strange pet, but he had no doubt that it would soon return to its wild, free kindred. In this, however, he was wrong, for the bird had evidently learnt that its present life suited it very well. It even seemed that it had lost all desire to fly, for the days passed and still it walked and jumped and hobbled as before, only occasionally using its wings to go out by the window or to gain some elevated perch. Yet the wing seemed sound and hard, and the owl could use it liberally and ably enough if it came to a tiff with the cat. Apparently it was merely a matter of existing circumstances having removed all need and desire to fly.

Things went on peacefully enough till winter came, and with the first snow and frost a change was noticeable in Jeff's pet. Though it need have known no hunger, it now took to hunting farther afield, and if Jeff was out after dark, it was more than likely that on his return the lights of the gig would reveal the huge, luminous eyes and the small dark outline of the bird seated on the white gate by the main road. There it would remain, humping its back and flapping its wings, and uttering its wheezy calls of greeting, while Jeff opened the gate and closed it behind him. But invariably by the time he had unharnessed, the owl was sitting waiting for him on the back of his easy chair. So Jeff proudly told his wife that he believed " yon bird recognized the step of the old Galloway as soon as they were clear of the village ".

Just before Christmas Jeff had to go away to mind the flocks of a brother who was sorely ill, and of course he took his dog with him. During his absence the owl behaved so strangely that Mrs. Jeff, who was an ailing and nervous woman, became afraid of it. It seemed to be out at elbows with everyone, and was so ill-tempered that it would not even allow the cat inside the kitchen. Once it flew at Mrs. Jeff's hand and drew blood when she tried to brush it aside, but she forgave it on the strength of her belief that the bird missed the master, as she herself did.

4

"It sits there and stares and stares at me wi' its twae big e'en, till I feel I could run and scream," she told a neighbour one day; to which the other woman replied, "I'd soon sort the varmint! Why d'ye no close the window on it?"

"Waur than useless," replied Mrs. Anderson. "He'd scuffle up against the glass and warble and hiss till he drove me silly! I'll be glad when Jeff comes hame, and next time he gangs awa', he maun tak' his bird wi' him."

That very evening, however, Mrs. Anderson had reason to change her views, for she had just lighted the candle to ascend to bed when a heavy step sounded on the cobbles outside, followed by an even heavier knock upon the door. She was, we have said, a nervous woman, and moreover she was quite alone, no telephone, no neighbours within a mile, so she inquired from the kitchen who was there.

"I've a message for ye, Mistress Anderson," came the reply, and the man's tone was so civil that though she did not recognize the voice, her misgivings were set at rest. She went and unlocked the door, but as her hand fell upon the latch it was thrust rudely open and a man's heavy boot inserted to prevent her closing it. Next moment she found herself looking into the unshaven face of the worst type of vagrant tinker, and as he leered at her the smell of strong liquor assailed her nostrils.

"I've come for ma supper," the man stated insolently. "As yer husband's awa' frae hame, the larder will nae doobt be weel stocked."

"Ye'll get nae supper here," replied Mrs. Anderson, striving gamely to disguise the fear in her voice. " Ye ought tae be ashamed o' yersel' trying tae scare a body this time o' nicht."

" There's nae call for ye tae be scared," replied the visitor naïvely. " I'll no herm ye, sae long as ye dae ma bidding. Woman, ye aught tae be pleased tae help a starving fellow mortal a nicht like this."

" I'll no be pleased tae help ye wi' yer cowardly insolence!" Mrs. Anderson retorted, but it was of no use, since the man had already forced his way into the lobby and was groping the grimy cap from his unkempt hair. Mrs. Anderson, almost swooning, went back to the kitchen, and the ruffian followed her.

" If I gie ye yer meat, will ye gang and no come back?" she demanded querulously; to which the man replied in tones which sounded anything but binding—" Aye, meat and baccy, and mebbe a pint o' beer."

" I've nae beer and baccy," she flung back at him. " Ye should have stayed at the Public if ye wanted thae things."

" A wee dram 'll no gang amiss, then," the man conceded insolently.

" Nor whisky naither," said Mrs. Anderson, obviously weakening.

The tinker glared at her, and a nasty look came into his narrow eyes. " That's a lie, onyway," he asserted. " Ye'll no tell me that Jeff Anderson hasna a pickle spirit for his freends. You get aboot finding the victuals, and I'll find the liquor."

At this Mrs. Anderson shrieked. She was on the

point of swooning, and staggered over to open the little window, almost falling against the sink. The ruffian caught her in his arms. Mrs. Anderson thrust him away, her eyes flaming.

" Keep yer hands off me, you brute!" she cried. " Ye'll gang tae prison for this, mark my words! I'll tak' guid care that ye're punished, ye evil creature!"

Somewhat abashed at her fury, the man cast himself luxuriously into Jeff's chair, while Mrs. Anderson flung some food on the table.

" Eat it and gang!" she demanded, and just then she caught sight of two huge eyes glaring in at the window. It was, of course, the owl, which had alighted noiselessly, and was now staring at the back of the grizzled head of the uninvited guest. The bird was craning its neck in a peculiar manner, as though unable to make out the general atmosphere of strangeness in the homely little room. For Mrs. Anderson it was but a fleeting vision, for again the the man was glaring at her.

" Where's that wee dram?" he demanded savagely.

" There's nae dram for ye," she answered.

" Is there no?" At this he rose to his feet. " I ken weel there's a bottle somewhere in the hoose, and if ye'll no get it for me, I'll need tae help myself!"

Mrs. Anderson fully realized that she had a desperate character to deal with, and the man was, moreover, already tipsy. To anger him would be but folly, and for a moment it occurred to her that if she gave him the bottle he might drink himself stupid and she would be able to slip away to the neighbours. But—what if the liquor did not have the desired effect? What if it merely made him more reckless and desperate? Given food, men of his type can often carry unlimited liquor, so Mrs. Anderson fell back upon the truth, leaving the rest in the lap of the gods.

"The spirit's in the parlour, safe in the locker, and the maister has the key wi' him," she stated.

At this the man uttered a chuckle of mirth. "Thae lockers are no sae hard tae break open," he asserted, turning towards the door.

"Suit yersel', then," replied Mrs. Anderson, "but if ye damage yon locker, ye'll have hoosebreaking up against ye in addition tae a' the rest. Ye need tae bear that in mind."

But the conversation got no further than this, for at that precise moment something which might have been a wild-cat shot in at the open window, and even before the ruffian could turn, it smote his face. Two clawed hands gripped and held, and with a roar of pain and bewilderment, the man struck out wildly. The owl somehow evaded the blow, then attacked again with such fury that Mrs. Anderson was frightened.

She had no idea that their pet could prove so formidable a customer, but the crux of the whole matter lay in the fact that the bird had got in first blow, and that blow was a terrible one. The man was down on his knees, blubbering: groaning, pawing at his eyes, apparently unable to defend himself further, while quite unaccountably Mrs. Anderson found herself armed with a dish cloth, driving out her deliverer.

"My e'en! My e'en!" the man was crying. "It's blinded me! I canna see!"

"A richt guid thing, tae!" cried Mrs. Anderson unmercifully.

"Where's the door? Let me oot!" groaned the visitor, rising to his feet and groping along the table. The blood was streaming copiously down his face.

"Aye, I'll dae that wi' spirit!" replied the lady of the house, and ten seconds later her uninvited guest was staggering over the cobbles, blubbering and groaning as he went.

Very early next morning a man who had been picked up on the road dazed and lost, though whether by drink or his wounds it was difficult to decide, was taken to the police station at a neighbouring village. His story was not coherent, but the doctor announced that he had evidently been attacked by some bird or beast. One of his eyes was pierced and the sight gone for all time, and in any case, Mrs. Anderson's uninvited guest was now in proper hands.

As for Jeff's owl, it never returned to the kitchen after that night, and Mrs. Jeff says, a shade remorsefully, that it is because she "drove him oot wi' the dish cloot!" Still, he occasionally meets Jeff at the gate, and almost every evening he sits on the roof of the house and warbles, and if Jeff calls him forth from the cobwebs of the barn in the early morning, he is "no agin" a saucerful of milk alongside the cat.

BURGOMASTER OF THE OCEAN WASTES

On a flat low-lying island of the Barents Sea, Burgomaster broke from the shell of the great brown egg, and proceeded to take for granted the glare of the Arctic world. Nothing green grew on that island, but it was dotted with pools and lagoons from the recently thawed snow, and overhead and all around was an incredible host of seabird life. There were waders by the million—knots, and turnshoes and sanderlings, and passing bands of phalaropes—such flocks of the lesser longshore birds as darkened the sky like a smoke screen; there were gulls great and small, pink-footed geese and white-fronted geese, and whooper swans, and Bewick's swans and scaup and king eiders, while the din of their voices filled heaven and earth, so that one would have heard them far out at sea. Day and night this bewildering din and activity never ceased, for there was now no darkness in that far land, only the blinding glare of the north, while the sea was the palest, coldest green, crested with snow-white runners, which bore the steely tinkle of ice.

Of this vast host of sea birds, probably not five per cent were nesting, albeit the nests were packed so closely that much of the noise came from the squabbling neighbours, for truly it was a world of strife. For the most part the different colonies kept

together, but it was noteworthy that, surrounding
the nest in which Burgomaster was born, there was
an empty circle, their nearest neighbours being a
pair of Great Iceland gulls, only a little smaller than
Burgomaster's parents, and well able to guard their
own interests.

It is customary to regard our gulls as fish feeders
who wring their livings from the sea, but Burgo's
parents, who measured close upon thirty inches
from beak-tip to tail-tip, knew of an easier way, and
only occasionally did they take the trouble to spread
their hawk-like wings and fly. For why work for a
living when there was plenty on every side?—when
one need do no more than stroll here and there and
watch for an unguarded nest, then gobble its contents, eggs or young, or perhaps, seize up some
sleeping Arctic tern, or golden plover, shake it as a
terrier shakes a rat, and carry it home to be served
up piecemeal to the chicks? Such was the parentage
from which Burgomasters spring—pirates of the
sea, highwaymen of the land, and, like most of the
greater gulls, so cordially hated by the other wild
fowl that one wonders why, there in their thousands,
they did not unite to be quit of the undesirables.

Of this great assembly, quite the majority were
immature birds, not even mated, yet true to their
instincts of migration they had returned to the
island of their birth as the sun sped north. But the
island had another charm. Here in the wastes of the
sea there was fresh water, which all gulls love, and
which the lesser migrants must have. Every pool
was covered with birds, spreading their wings and

enjoying their freshwater ablutions—fresh, that is, in so far as it was not salt. Every pool, indeed, was foul and fetid, for the sun was now hot, and daily the ponds were thickening as their level sank. But it was this oasis in the desert which drew the phala-rope thousands, and the multitudes of others who came this way across the wastes to drink.

But apart from the social life of his native isle, which does not really concern this story; there was not much incident attached to Burgomaster's early days, so let us go forward to the morning when, late that summer, he got up and waddled sedately from the nest amidst loud applause from his parents. He was now fully fledged, but his plumage was not the beautiful pale pearl and snowy white of his parents, though the bars and mottlings of brown about his breast were pale for an immature gull, and his white parts were snowy white. Indeed, he was very plainly a creature of the Arctic, but by now the promiscuous rabble had fled from the island, and only the larger gulls, whose chicks were slow in maturing, remained. For weeks past the sea had been crowded with bird life all round the island as more chicks and yet more took to the waves, but the fresh water was all but gone, and ere long the island would be barren, deserted, ready for another winter's snows.

So young Burgomaster waddled out across the sands and into the sea, and—oh, the joy of it! How he raised his head and cackled and croaked to his parents with strong goose-like notes, while eagerly they jostled round him, for he was their first chick. So he bade the island farewell, and for many weeks now, perhaps for many months, Burgomaster might not again alight on land, for he was essentially a bird of the high seas. So his life began.

Gulls in thousands still dotted these Arctic waters, and Burgo had inherited a good deal of knowledge in the art of keeping alive. He was mainly a surface feeder, and when his parents saw a great gathering of gulls at one particular point, they would hasten there, urging Burgo to follow them. At first he was reluctant to try to fly, then came a strong wind, and when his parents called to him and mounted, he spread his great wings, and behold! The wind got under them and up he glided—up and up with scarcely an effort of his own, then the prodigious wheel and stoop and the headlong plunge down-wind. The glory of flight was his!

With that came independence, yet he and his parents remained united. They were ever watchful for the shoals of surface fish, betrayed by the other gulls—indeed, on clear days, the three of them would mount to the topmost heavens and glide and circle, watching as the vultures watch. Soon, far off, they would mark a cyclone of feeding gulls, then down, slantwise across the heavens at prodigious speed, to feed as the other gulls were feeding by snatching the tiny fish from the surface, or if they were too deep, to watch for the diving gulls and assault them for their catch as they broke surface. Always they were on the look-out for weaker birds with food, and had you seen these three great gulls, the two snowy white, the third barred and mottled with brown, measuring forty-two inches from wing-tip to wing-tip, you might have mistaken them for white buzzards, for both in shape and in their powers of flight they resembled the birds of prey.

Then came the first storm of autumn, when the wind rose to a fury which drove the Burgomasters from the surface of the sea. Well they knew it was coming, and night found Burgo and his parents high in the heavens, sailing idly on rigid wings, and seemingly in perfect calm. All round was the moon-light and the stars, and far below shone the silver linings of the clouds, all torn and rolling and tor-tured by the gale. Up there it was blowing too, but the great gulls were soaring with the wind. They soared in mighty circles with wings rigid, one after the other, " chock-chocking " to each other as they flew—falling and gaining speed as they fled on the wings of the gale, mounting as they turned to meet it, then round and away again. The clouds were moving with them, so that they kept no count of the mighty distances they swept that night—over sea and land perhaps, and lakes and sunny ranges, these children of the distances.

At dawn they descended through the drenching, driving mists, but there was no living down there in the chaos where sea and gale seemed to unite, so up again, into the sunlight, and still on and away, and when next the moon shone, each great gull had its head buried at intervals in the feathers of its back, sleeping as it flew.

This was the first great test of the young gull's life. All round him in the wastes of sky and sea other young gulls of the high seas, which are those which seek the uppermost heavens rather than the land, were similarly undergoing their test. Thousands would fail and go fluttering down, to be beaten and wrecked by the fury of the ocean storm, till their numbers ridged the shores of lonely islands, but always the storms seem to abate before the fittest of the fit descend.

We see now why the great gulls had fled *with* the wind, for had they tried to battle against it they would soon have fallen exhausted, and now for sixty hours they had glided thus. Young Burgo was hungry and weary beyond all endurance. Always he seemed to be planing down, losing height, reluctant to rise—always his parents flew above him with their strong, reassuring, cackling notes. Then for a time the gale ceased, and they descended to the bosom of the sea and slept there, riding mountains high, but soon it was blowing again, bidding them rise. There followed days of this kind of thing— brief breaks in the storm, then another furious spell, and if the gulls knew now where they were, their sense of direction was beyond understanding. Once, on descending, they sighted a great cargo boat, making heavy weather of it indeed, but till nightfall they followed her with the attendant fulmers, even hanging under the shelter of her spray-drenched superstructure, yet they did not alight. A morsel of refuse snatched from the spume-swept sea, then night and the fury of the storm again, and up and up, till the steamer's lights vanished far below.

When finally the storm spell lifted, the three great gulls were little more than bone and feathers, yet it would seem that for all those hundreds of miles of circling, with not even the stars as possible guidance, they knew exactly where they were. No land was in sight, yet they bore towards the north-west, and below were other gulls, flying with them, snowflakes in the space beneath. Thus, in the dusk of evening, many little lights twinkled below, and downwards they swooped, to be met by a host of gulls, such as had thronged the island. For here was food in abundance and shelter from the storms— a mid-ocean stronghold of the Burgomasters, for they are truly scavengers of the wastes. So Burgo descended to feed as he had never fed before, for here was the unlimited refuse which the Arctic whaling station had cast aside, to be gleaned by the ravenous hosts of gulls, without whom the station would truly have become uninhabitable.

Burgomaster stayed there through the winter, roosting on the bosom of the sea, but he lost track of his parents in the seagull host, whose screaming never ceased through the long, dark months; till a savage brightening in the south each day at noon told him that Old Sol was journeying north again. And there in the crimson and gold of what was both dawn and sunset, Burgomaster and a thousand other gulls climbed heavenwards, till the wastes of white-ness below, streaked with the dark and stormy arms of the sea, were hidden in the darkening.

Truly could these great gulls be called the chil-dren of the storms, the waifs of the ocean winds. Burgomaster was among the world's greatest travel-lers, but it was the wind which bore him, soaring

in gigantic circles, sometimes drifting across the
wind as he soared, so that the west wind might bear
him north-east or south-east, but always gliding
idly. Already he had seen the two hemispheres, and
the glare of spring had begun when one day he
swooped towards a little island, dotted with freshwater pools, and already white with gulls. Many
immature gulls of his own kind were there, together
with their snowy elders, but Burgo did not seek a
mate, and he stayed only a little while. This was
perhaps because the cold north wind bore a message
of wanderlust, for, having fed savagely on the eggs
and young of the smaller sea fowl, he took to the
heavens once more, ready now for many days of
travelling ere he would need to feed again.

That spring Burgo drifted about the rim of the
Arctic circle. Spitzbergen he knew, then across the
wastes to Iceland, and still by Cape Farewell to
Baffin Bay. He came to know the whaling stations
and the seaport towns, and where the fishing fleets
gather at the appointed seasons, and that little compass in his brain never failed, though often he slept
a-wing above the clouds, to waken, a hundred miles
away, with nothing but sea below.

Burgo returned to his native island again next
spring, and this time he stayed several weeks, though
again he did not mate. Yet while he was there he
shed the last of his ashen-brown feathers, and
donned the pearl and snowy whiteness of his adult
plumage, while his eyes lost their amber rings and
became pearly white—a cold, cruel, and expression-
less colourlessness, born of the Arctic glare.

Thereafter we cannot follow all his wanderings. He took to accompanying the vessels of the sea, and because of his powers of sustained flight, that habit alone might have seen him across the world. Summer found him in the Fair Isles, and that October Burgomaster was seated serenely on a chimney-pot in the little fishing village of Eyeport. He had dallied in his journey south at Aberdeen, Montrose, and even at the Port of Leith, whence he had circled at dusk over "The City of the Crags", and citizens who had looked up from the grey streets at the flight of soaring gulls, pink in the autumn sunset, had never paused to think of the regions from which they might have come, of the dim and desolate lands they might have known, of the storms and the Arctic majesty of winter, and of moonlight and starlight above the storms, in a world so wonderfully different from our own that it becomes hard to believe that such can exist.

So, one evening, a visitor to the steep little village of Eyeport, looking down over the chimney-pots and the harbour, with its boats at rest, remarked to a fisherman: "There's a bad one there, John!"

He indicated a great white gull on a chimney-pot below—a very beautiful creature in its snowy whiteness, with its mother-of-pearl eyes.

"I ken," agreed the villager. "He's no' a good yin onyway."

"I was watching him through my glasses ten minutes ago," said the visitor. "He picked up a dunbie down on the shore there, gave it a shake, and swallowed it whole! A charge of number four

HE HAD CIRCLED AT DUSK OVER "THE CITY OF THE CRAGS"

shot would be the best thing for him—one of the Bolshies of the bird world!"

" Na-na," said the seaman, as he strolled away, his hands in his trouser pockets. He looked back, and removed his pipe. "Na-na!" he repeated. " You must no' shoot a Burgomaster gull!"

A few nights later a sea fog drifted in from the open sea, and piled itself in dense wreaths under the cliffs. The foghorns roared here and there while the little fleet, returning from its lifelong search for haddies, groped slowly inland through the dense and drenching mists. At the harbour mouth a group of old men and women and children stood waiting anxiously, while out at sea they could hear the surf booming on the reefs.

"Can ye no' show a light!" shouted the fisherman at the wheel of the leading boat. He, if anyone, could bring the fleet safely back to harbour.

" What's wrong wi' the light?" answered his brother from the gloom below. " A light's nae use till it comes to picking up our moorings! We're heading straight for Schoolhouse Point, so I'm telling ye!"

" Dear knows where we're heading!" replied the helmsman candidly. " Show a light for'ard! There's a Burgomaster hanging straight over our boom. Show a light on him, and I'll follow him in! I ken yon muckle gull!"

So the other man moved forward, and centred the beam of his electric torch on the great white gull, which hung, like a ghost of the sea, gliding on

5

rigid wings just ahead of them, occasionally circling off, then returning to the same place, flying by the familiar line which the fleet always took to the harbour mouth; and so to the grey stone piers where the lights shone, true as a compass point, led the Burgomaster, the pilot gull, one whose bearings never faltered, fog or storm, and in whose brain was an infallible little needle, which took no reckoning from stars or beacons or landmarks. So when all else fails, he will guide you home.

Late that winter Burgo circled northwards, along by the trail of the wild swans and the little auks. How long he lived I do not know. I can only say that from October till after Christmas, every year for nearly half a man's lifetime, that great white glaucous gull was to be seen, at certain hours of the day, serenely resting on his chosen chimney-pot in the village of the many terraces. Then came the memorable spring when even the gannets were beaten down from the uppermost heavens—storm after storm which took such toll of the birds of the high seas that many who were formerly abundant, failed to show themselves from the Arctic wastes for long, long after. I saw no Burgomaster gulls about the seaport towns that autumn. They were among the missing, for—of such the fury of the sea! Even the Burgomasters were gone!

THE FIGHTING PLANES

I

In the rugged face of Mount-o'-Cairn, a hundred feet from the brow of the cliff and three hundred feet from the surf below, the three little peregrines were hatched. Nest there was none, only a hollow scraped out in the sandy shelf, and so overhung by the ledge above that they were shielded from sun and rain, and—most important of all—from human eyes, and the missiles of death certain humans might have showered upon them. To such cliffs as Mount-o'-Cairn the peregrine owes its scant survival; for here, about those towering shelves, the rocks were set in crumbling sand, so that even the alighting of a gull might set a landslide moving. For the human spoiler, then, the nest was inaccessible.

One had only to see that place to know that here, if anywhere, the peregrine might be found, for with its scowling grandeur and its inexpressible solitude, it was a fitting place for the fittest of our birds of prey. Rugged in character, peregrines love such rugged haunts, and for centuries past they had bred in Mount-o'-Cairn. Year after year they returned to this stronghold, and at one time the peregrines of that cliff were reserved for the kings of Scotland. Those days are long since gone, and from the lofty position the peregrine then held he has sunk to the status of vermin. Yet the peregrines of Mount-o'-

Cairn still belong to the Crown, for the ancient law has never been rescinded.

They were not the only tenants of the place; indeed, they shared it with thousands of others— kittiwakes, lesser black-backed gulls, herring-gulls, fulmars, rock doves, and rabbits, while in the lower sea-washed caves, dingy and dripping, where no man had ever trod, a colony of shags had their nests, and could be seen coming and going like the business-like folk they are. No, the peregrines were not alone, but certainly they were aloft and aloof from the vulgar rabble on the shelves below.

The visitor to the place would at first see nothing of them, but presently he would hear a metallic rasping note, harsh and defiant, which he would know at once as the voice of a royal bird. Separate and apart it seemed to ring, while anon the gulls screamed and croaked, filling the air as they soared and glided about their nesting shelves, and below the surf thundered. Hollow booming sounds came up, stabbed now by a shriek as of a frightened woman, now by peal after peal of crazy laughter, and as a thousand gulls filled the air, dazzling the eyes as they flashed in the sunshine, there, behold, was milord, gliding in immeasurable space!

He was not difficult to locate—a black darting speck, now sweeping skywards, now darting in and out amidst the giddy throng, cutting rings round the rest and making the swiftest of them slow by comparison. Moreover, he was rendered conspicuous by the fact that everywhere he went he was pursued by the vulgar crowd, first one, then another, plunging headlong after the master flyer; and when one of them came too near, the falcon would scream warningly as he swerved in his flight, then rise up, up, in colossal bounds.

This had gone on since the peregrines arrived several weeks previously, and now to-day the chicks were hatched. Within an hour of their hatching a man and a girl descended the green slope beyond the cliff to the ruins of the castle which jutted out on a headland. And there, with the face of Mount-o'-Cairn in view, they stayed awhile, watching the bird life. The tercel resented their presence, and was constantly a-wing. Now he would glide overhead, uttering his fierce harsh note, then seawards he would dive through the scintillating host, never failing to draw the angry mob in pursuit, but in a moment he was up and away. Then at intervals he would fly full tilt at the cliff, as though to dash himself lifeless; but, gaining his look-out shelf above the eyrie, he would stop dead and land—lightly as thistle-seed.

One big herring-gull, which evidently had its nest near to the falcon's shelf, was particularly persistent in its attacks upon him, and the man remarked to his companion—" That gull will go a little too far one of these days."

Exactly what happened the two people did not see, because it occurred just beyond their line of vision. That morning, I say, the chicks had left the eggs, which perhaps accounted for it, for hitherto the fighting planes had avoided dispute with the greater gulls.

When the two visitors finally left the headland and sauntered up the cliff they found, lying in a wash-out, at the end of a train of its own feathers, a great herring-gull, which looked almost the size of an albatross. Very beautiful it was in its spring-time plumage, and, as they raised the warm body in their hands, more feathers fell. They saw that the strong neck was almost severed, while the patch between the wide shoulders was denuded of feathers.

"How did it die?" The girl asked the question, for on account of its beauty she was sorry for the bird.

"Gulls," the man answered, "are the gangsters of the bird world."

"How was it killed?" the girl repeated, and presently her companion, turning to offer his hand on the steep ascent, answered indirectly—for he loved the peregrines—"If one were mobbed by a vulgar crowd every time on leaving one's ancestral home, it would surely be permissible if at length one knocked down the ring-leader?"

"It was the peregrine, then?" she demanded.

"I'm afraid so," he answered. "Yes, undoubtedly."

"What a pity that such beautiful things should be so cruel," she summed it up.

II

At first, when the chicks were very small, the tercel hunted for them and for his mate, while she protected her fluffy brood from the cold east winds, and from the chill sea damps, which for days on end smote the cliff face. One morning an artisan, going to his work at five in the morning (summer-time) down the High Street of the nearest market town, was surprised to see the pigeons rise from the square and fan up hastily into the church tower. But his surprise was short-lived, for now he beheld milord in blue, progressing along the High Street about a yard from the ground—so low, indeed, that his tapered wings cast up a little scurry of dust. He passed within five yards of the human observer, then suddenly he corkscrewed and pinwheeled skywards. Wheeling round the tower, he knocked the proudest, plumpest pigeon into giddy space. As it smote the cobbles and rebounded, the man ran forward to secure the prize for himself. His hands were within a yard of it, when the peregrine alighted on the dead bird. Seeing him, evidently for the first time, it uttered a shrill " kree " of surprise and defiance, and " sucked " up, under his very eyes. And there on the polished cobbles it left only a little heap of feathers.

The tercel's look-out tower on Mount-o'-Cairn was high above the eyrie, to which he rarely descended. Cutting the air above, his prey in his talons, he would utter a cackling call, then let fall his lifeless load. And as it fell through space, the hen bird would launch herself from the eyrie, turn keel upwards, and catch the prize in mid-air, to dart back instantly to her young.

Soon, however, the demands of the chicks were too great for the tercel to cope with, and since the weather had improved, the hen bird left them at intervals to feed herself and to bring back food for them. So ere long both parents were a-wing from dawn till dusk, and many a hundred leagues they flew. Once or twice the hen bird, which was the larger—her wings designed for greater lifting power —returned to the eyrie with a hen ptarmigan, and the nearest ptarmigan height was thirty miles away. Plovers, pigeons, puffins, teal, and once a young brown hare, were brought and laid beside the chicks to devour at their leisure; and sometimes, after sunset, when the sky was still aglow and the sea was clear, and the thunder of the surf and the cries of the gulls seemed to enhance, rather than to break, the mighty quietude, both falcons would soar upwards into the blue—up, up, till the gossamer clouds were reached, and they were the merest specks in the unlimited glory of space. Then, as though for the joy of it, they would drop to earth in a sheer, unbroken plunge, swift as thunderbolts, to wheel and scream and sweep and glide, scattering wide the gulls, finally to alight, the tercel on his look-out shelf, the hen bird by her brood.

Once two wild ducks came wheeling round the headland, two hundred feet or more from the surface of the sea, and the human spectator watched, knowing now that the band would play. The ducks were flying down-wind, swift even for their kind, and the man saw the hen peregrine shoot from her shelf. Down she came towards the ducks, straight down. They swerved and quacked and doubled in the air, but too late! There was a heavy thud, and one was

THEY SWERVED AND QUACKED AND DOUBLED IN THE AIR

spinning seawards in a cloud of its own feathers.
The other dived headlong, straight down into the
sea, and so escaped with its life. But the peregrine
did not descend for the duck that she had killed.
She left it floating on the surface, and in a minute or
so a hundred screaming gulls descended upon it.
When at last they rose from the surface there was
no trace left of the peregrine's kill.

I have said that sometimes the hen falcon visited
the distant ptarmigan hill, and one evening on the
lower slopes of that hill the keeper was busy digging
peats when he heard a swish of wings above his
head. He looked up to see a hen peregrine descending—not in a straight nose-dive, after the manner of
her kind, but at an angle of forty-five degrees across
the glen. He turned for his gun, but she was far out
of range ere his fingers reached it. The keeper saw
her alight in the heather about a hundred yards
away. She seemed puzzled, for she sat there looking
about her, and meantime the keeper, armed now,
quickly stole up. He knew very well that the falcon
had descended in pursuit of a covey of grouse in
the heather she had seen from afar, and that the
grouse had huddled down, hiding themselves as she
approached. As the man came up, he saw the hen
falcon walking about, looking for her prey. He saw
her suddenly strike her armed feet deep into the
ling roots, and next moment she would have been
a-wing but that—the keeper fired.

He fired—yes, and killed. So there was yet
another little freebooter less, no more to take her
deadly toll, nor yet to delight the heart of man by

her wonderful powers. When he got up she lay very still, her wonderful wings outspread, her claws still fast upon the grouse she had struck deep down in the ling. And from the man's very feet five more grouse rose, to skim the ling-tips scarcely a foot from the ground, then to pitch again and bury themselves not twenty yards away.

The keeper laughed. This had been a lucky day for him, for it was not often a peregrine came his way; and from that day on it has been the man's boast that he is the only keeper who has ever shot a peregrine hunting its prey on foot.

III

That evening the tercel lingered long in the sunset glory, rising and wheeling, calling, calling—those sharp metallic notes, to which no answer came. Till after darkness the sound rang above the bedlam of the gulls, and when she did not come, the tercel seemed to understand, because he descended to guard his chicks from the chill sea wind.

Possibly she was not the first mate he had lost, for in this land of ours the life of such as the peregrine is one of hourly peril. He has many friends, but they cannot show their friendship by defending him from his foes—and his foes are everywhere. So one day the tercel himself would fall, unless those wings bore him to some far-off land where the boom of the shot-gun never breaks the mountain quietude.

There was no keeping pace with the growing

hunger of those chicks, and before the first dawn-light till darkness closed upon the sea, he was a-wing. He fed them largely on puffins, which were nesting in thousands about a cliff only two miles away, though it was often remarked that the pigeons in the neighbouring town were perceptibly decreasing in numbers. It was said that the tercel came before there was sufficient light to see things clearly, and, indeed, there were grounds for this belief, for almost every morning a litter of pigeon feathers lay upon the cobbles down below the church clock.

Be that as it may, the peregrine ably carried on the task which was now his lot in life.

A little varmint! Yes, yet true to his colours—royal blue, touched with the ermine of kings.

The young peregrines soon left the nest, and, able to fly a few feet, they moved from shelf to shelf. This, if anything, increased the tercel's labours, for he could locate them only by their cries, and since each of the three screamed its loudest every time he appeared, he had no way of telling which was the hungriest—which he had fed last. But this diffi-culty soon solved itself, for one of the chicks, falling, alighted at length on a great rocky outcrop fifty yards out at sea. Another succeeded in gaining the castle ruins, and took up its perch on the topmost pinnacle thereof, while the third, the least adven-turous, remained near to the eyrie. Thus the tercel knew them by their positions, and fed them each in turn.

Another two or three days and the young falcons were a-wing with their parent. It was a pretty sight to see them circling after him—clumsy, indeed, compared with his supreme mastery of the air, though already there was a gliding ease and swiftness in their flight which marked them out amidst the glistening horde. Up and up they climbed, the tercel encouraging them to follow by his shrill calls overhead, till soon all four were the merest specks in the sky. Then the tercel disappeared, and there were only three. Soon there was only one, and he, too, was going—going—gone. All were lost now in the eternal glare, from which they did not return and so we must leave them—lost in the infinite space to which they belonged.

The following day a strange thing happened. It was a Sunday—a clear, breathless Sabbath morn; and at the appointed hour the inhabitants of the little market town filed along the hot sidewalk to the parish church. Soon the bells ceased to clang, and, save for the hushed and intermittent droning of the organ, there was no sound about those grey walls, with their stained-glass windows.

Aloft on the weather-vane a jackdaw sat idly chipping his comrades as they scurried by in shuffling flight; but all at once the jackdaw let go his hold and fell, as though shot, from his lofty perch. He simply let himself fall, ricochetting down the ancient tower, from tile to draining spout, then down again, calling wildly as he fell, to the very vestry porch. Then through the open doors he hopped, into that quiet shady place, and the old minister, looking up, saw the bird enter by the aisle, to seek sanctuary at last beside the font. So, indeed, have others, less worthy than God's wild children, sought sanctuary in their hour of need.

When the good citizens came out of church they found a little knot of people standing out in the High Street gazing up at the wind-vane, impaled on the topmost spike of which, and moving limply in the wind, was the body of a bird with long tapered wings. Someone said it was a falcon, that he had seen it descend from the blue in pursuit of a jackdaw, which had fallen to earth in the ace of time.

Later the old beadle went up to remove the body, which was no easy task, since the spike had passed clean through it, and was bent almost double by the impact. Taking the bird in his hands, he was surprised at its lightness. Indeed, it weighed only a few ounces, and the man held in his hand a mere shattered pulp of skin and bone—a beautiful bird all the same, though the lustre of the feathers had already faded. Later the taxidermist announced, " Starved! Possibly a piner, possibly a migrant. At all events, there's nothing but bone and sinews left of him."

The why and the wherefore of which only those who had found the dead herring-gull, and who had watched the falcons day by day could have told.

THE ALIENS

The last lights of sunset were fading over a stormy sky as the starlings alighted—hundreds of them, till the old dead tree was crowded, branch and twig, and there they struck up their ragtime chorus, which is the clown's band of bird music. All the same, there was a buoyant cheeriness in their discord, and it was as though the old stark tree had suddenly become hung with bells, which, like the harp of Æolis, gave forth music as the wind smote them.

All day the forests had shaken their wet limbs to the wild March wind, but it was spring by the calendar, and now, with the darkening, there was a taste of spring in the air. Perhaps that was why there was so much bustle and stir among the starlings—for the great pack which had stood united all winter was breaking up! In ones and twos, even in little batches, they were leaving the parent body, scattering out across the woods, and at last the discord faded to the merest twitter, for of all that vast gathering only two starlings remained in the old dead tree, and those two were side by side on the topmost branch.

It was almost dark now, and at length one of them rose and flew off, closely followed by the other. Not far did they fly, for the old dead tree stood at the edge of the walnut grove, which was a starling's paradise of nesting nooks and corners. They were very old walnuts, and the leading starling alighted on a limb of one of the sturdiest, then, as though she knew the place, dived immediately into a hole in the decaying trunk, and her mate followed with characteristic decision. So night came, but spring was now upon the land.

Next morning both starlings were busy flying back and forth between the walnut and the old dead tree, from the bearded branches of which they were dragging the lichen for the foundation of their nest. It was not to be much of a nest, merely a little roughly-lined hollow down in the dark trunk, just so far from the entrance hole that a boy, reaching in, could not quite have touched it. There was plenty of room inside that hollow trunk for a dozen starlings to nest, but the two had already claimed it, and forthwith proceeded to challenge any other starling which dared to go anywhere near.

They were not, however, to be left in undisputed possession, for at dusk four evenings later, when the nest was complete and contained one pale-blue egg, there was a scratching on the bark outside, for a huge old mother house rat was climbing up to the starlings' entrance.

Then pandemonium broke loose, as well it might, for the wild birds have just about as much cause to trust the alien [1] rats as to trust cats or weasels. Both parent starlings flew around the mother rat, screaming murder, actually striking her with their wings, but up she climbed, clinging to the rough bark with

[1] The house rat came from the Baltic early in the seventeenth century.

her small naked hands, steadily nearer and nearer to
the hole. Meantime, other starlings, hearing the
outcry, came up to help discourage the unwelcome
stranger; a wren and a blackbird joined in the
general discord, but the mother rat climbed heedlessly on. She did not pause to dispute the matter;
she simply proceeded with the task on hand, giving
neither ear nor eye to the noisy mob which would
have thwarted her, and so eventually she reached
that very hole and scratched and slithered down
through the darkness within.

Now the starlings were in a dilemma, for on the
face of things it would surely be madness to proceed
with their nesting affairs under the eye of such a
lodger. Yet they were there first, and this was the
spring, and mothers the world over observe certain
rules where spring is concerned. It has to be so, of
course, for where would the weaker folk come in if
none could rear its young near the thresholds of the
strong? So the wee wren may share a hollow log
with the owl, the mouse may rear her young amongst
the twigs of the buzzard's eyrie, and the dove may
lay her pearl-white eggs under the very eye of the
nesting hawk.

Anyway, those starlings made no bones about it,
though for the next day or two there was generally
a bit of a shindy in the hollow tree each dawn and
dusk, when the big rat came and went. Presently
even this ceased, though had one examined the
entrance hole closely one would have seen the marks
of muddy paws about the bark, leading in a distinct
footpath to the branch below, then down again by

6

the way the big mother rat always came and went. She must, on each occasion, have passed within an inch or two of the starling sitting her eggs—five in number now—for the rat had been very busy scratching and shaping out a nest three feet or so lower down in the darkness.

Each time she came and went the starling would open her beak and hiss at her as she brushed past, but that old rat observed the law, and continued to take not the least notice of her fellow-lodgers. She, indeed, was here for the summer, and from the manner in which she seemed to know her way about it was not the first time she had forsaken the farm steading to spend the days of sunshine in those rural quarters.

One morning a faint, thin-edged squeaking came up through the darkness from the lower flat, and the mother starling, cocking her head awry and listening, seemed to understand. An hour later squeakings came from the upper flat also, and a little while later both starlings might have been seen carrying broken egg-shells from the nest and flying over the wood to drop the tell-tale fragments there. So the little starlings were born—so also the little rats, and of them there were eleven!

It seemed that there was quite a neighbourly feeling now, for sometimes the tenants would meet at the very door, the starlings always coming and going. If they met Mrs. Rat there they would simply flutter aside an inch or two, leaving her to push past with her usual blind indifference. Indeed, it was not very long before something happened whereby the birds were made very glad of their neighbours' presence.

About those walnut trees there had often sounded of late, particularly at dawn and dusk, a strange flute-like whistling, which somehow had about it a foreign accent. The bird voices of our land vary greatly, yet all of them seem to speak the English tongue. This bird note, for such indeed it was, was not quite English—it was, in fact, the call of a Little Owl,[1] attracted to the walnut grove by the noise of the many young starlings whose prolonged " chee-ee " came from almost every nook.

So one evening, while there was yet light enough, the big-headed, big-eyed little foreigner peered in through the entrance hole—straight down and into the face of Mrs. Starling, who was just arranging herself over her chicks for the night. To say that she was alarmed would be putting it mildly, for those were terrible eyes, luminous, remorseless, cat-like.

Poor Mrs. Starling could do but one thing—stay where she was and shriek; and shriek she truly did, while without rang the terrified cries of her husband. Then the terrible head came through a little farther, and in a moment the feathered cat would have been down upon her, but——

Below there sounded a vicious, saw-edge scream, plaintive, yet fierce, full of shuddering cowardice, yet bearing all the bravery of desperation, a sound which has no counterpart in Nature, the scream of a

[1] Imported to various parts of England as a vermin killer. Its daylight habits have given good cause to doubt its all-round usefulness.

cornered rat. Up she came, all teeth and claws, scrambling over the terrified starling—up without faltering to meet that dreadful guest in the narrow passageway. There was a thud and a hiss, and for a moment the rat hung back, hunched and taut, then something seemed to break, and Mrs. Rat fell back in a shower of fur and feathers. But the light was shining through the entrance hole again, the dreadful face was gone, and far off there sounded that flute-like whistle, accompanied by the angry chattering of the father starling as he convoyed the routed trespasser back to the woodland edge.

Thus the grey lodger proved a friend indeed, but all the same one cannot pretend that outside her own door she was very much better than the Little Owl. Often, at dead of night, there sounded a frenzied twittering of starlings or tree sparrows from the nooks near by, and even the jackdaws complained that their eggs were disappearing. This creature, indeed, who was nursing her young beside a clamouring brood, was living on eggs and chicks in the shadowy nooks, for she could climb like a squirrel; yet here, in her own den, the old, old law of live and let live held.

It was about this time that a strange grey caterpillar began to appear about the branches of the walnut tree, which truly would have borne neither leaves nor nuts had these pests been left unchecked. At first there were only a few, then they were creeping everywhere, and the starlings had need to fly no farther than their own threshold to feed their chicks.

The Aliens

We hear much of the destructiveness of the house rats, but of the good they do we hear little, because there is so little to tell. One night, however, a very strange scene might have been witnessed about that old walnut tree, for it seemed that the mother rat must have told her neighbours about the succulent caterpillar feast, and there they were, scores of them, whirling their tails and climbing from twig to twig to the very tips of the branches.

All night they did trapeze work, seeking even the topmost shoots, and what became of those caterpillars no one ever knew. The gardeners said that a sharp frost, lasting only a few minutes at daybreak, must have killed them, and least of all would they have credited the rats; yet the rats are all wise, and next autumn they would come again in their scores to rob the tree of its nuts, as for many autumns past, and so to garner their hoards against the cold days of winter. Thus, wheels within wheels, there would have been no harvest that autumn had the insect pest continued, though to what extent all that was reasoned out we cannot, of course, know.

All the young rodents and the young starlings throve apace, for that was a rich land, and it was not long before the chicks began to show a desire to gain the point of light above. The baby rats were even more ambitious, and so it came about that one morning, when the mother rat was out, the mother starling returned to her noisy brood to find a baby rat clinging desperately to the bark just outside the entrance hole. Clearly this was all wrong, and the

starling mother, being a starling mother, set up
once more that wild, rasping screech for help she had
uttered when the Little Owl looked in.

The mother rat heard it, and came headlong
home, knowing not what kind of foe was invading
the starlings' door, which was her door, and so she
found her wayward child and caught him just before
he dropped. Thus—unwittingly no doubt—the
feathered mother repaid her furred and whiskered
neighbour some little of her debt.

Yet another day or two and the young birds took
their departure from the home cranny, to fly off
with their parents, whom they would accompany in
joyous insect hunts all that summer and autumn.
On the whole the strange nesting arrangement had
worked very well for all concerned. But perhaps the
strangest incident of all in that strange alliance was
yet to come.

The little starlings were still foolish and feeble on
the wing, and the day. after they left the nest their
parents took them down to the shores of the little
lake at the grove end to drink. It had been a hot
day, and all were very thirsty. Before long, indeed,
even the little lake would be thirsty, for each day a
wider belt of muddy margin was cracking in the
sun. So the young birds were drinking when yet
another alien came into their lives—a grey squirrel [1]
from the forests of the south, beyond which, alas,
they were speedily spreading. This one seemed to

[1] Imported to various parts of England during the past century, it is speedily
ousting the red squirrel, as the house rat ousted the native black rat, and being
very carnivorous in its habits it is a doubtfully welcome importation.

come from nowhere in particular, for even the keen-eyed, anxious starling parents did not see him till they heard the frenzied screaming of their child.

Yes, there he was, holding the young bird down at the water's edge, for all the world like a little tiger. The other chicks flew off, but the parents flew at him, attacking him bravely, lashing his eyes with their wings, and—screaming.

Yes, screaming! The same old well-known starling scream which had called the big rat mother to defend her home against the alien owl—called her again when her little one was clinging to the bark, and now. She did not know, she could not have paused to think. She was spending much of her time at the water's edge herself these thirsty days, and so she was within earshot, and she came.

That same rasping, thin-edged screech, and in a moment they were together, squirrel and rat—rolling over and over, interlocked, so that one could not have told what the combatants were. It was a close fight in more than one sense. They fought for twenty minutes, inseparably embraced, and embracing they rested, fought, and rested again. In the trees all round, small birds were rasping and twittering as they watched, and once a big black poaching cat peered over the bank to see what it was all about, saw, and went away. But still they fought, till the keeper, hearing the bird voices and thinking there must be a fox or a cat in a trap, came over to the little lake to see.

As he came, the bird voices subsided, because the movements of the two combatants along the muddy

THE PARENTS FLEW AT HIM

margin of the lake were subsiding, so he lost their direction, and it was not until he was returning home that his attention was arrested by something at the water's edge. He thought in the half light that it was a hedgehog, but as he touched it with his foot one half went bounding off into the bushes near-by.

" Drat it!" said he. " That was a rat."

But the other half still lay very still at his feet, nor would it stir again, and he wondered why a rat and a squirrel should be clenched thus in mortal combat. He wondered, too, at the bedlam of starling voices in the old stark tree across the walnut grove. It was the wrong season of the year for the starlings to be in packs, yet there must have been scores of them assembled there to-night, holding some ritual according to the strange customs of their kind, as in the early days of spring.

" Must be a grey squirrel or a Little Owl disturbing them," said he to himself. " Or maybe a big rat. These old woods of mine are full of aliens!"

THE MASTER OF CAMOUFLAGE

Towards the open moor the wood gradually petered out, the pines becoming fewer and farther between as the heather deepened—such heather, since for many years it had known not the brand of the ling burner! Since the wood existed it had grown unchecked, till now it was of such depths that the roe deer could come and go along their runways without so much as showing an ear above the sage-like growth. It suited the deer, it suited Brock, the badger, but, most of all, it suited Cockabundle, the pheasant, for he, too, like the roe, had his secret and shadowy " creeps ", and all winter he had evaded shot and powder in the wood below by running like a hare for this sanctuary of the moorland edge. Here, too, under the peat banks, he had his sunning places, which, when all the rest of the world was dank and dripping, afforded dry and dusty couches, in which he rejoiced to sprawl and flutter.

Technically, winter was ended, yet at the altitude of the moor snow was everywhere, and the hungry ice teeth clung to the lips and ledges. To-day it was radiantly clear, and a million jewels sparkled in the pines. Cockabundle had his claws full. How he had become involved I do not know, for he was not in the habit of disagreeing with strangers, and why he did not make for the deep heather, and thus get out of the way, it is difficult to conjecture. Possibly it was because he dearly loved a fight!

The sparrowhawk was seated on the topmost limb of a stunted pine. His eyes were wild, his feathers ruffed out, and at the foot of that pine stood Cockabundle—vigorously scratching. Russet as a rowan he was, but as the high lights caught his plumage it flashed purple and green, while his wattles flushed vermilion as his fighting blood rose. Six times already the audacious hawk had " dabbed " at him, and Cockabundle, pretending to be absorbed in his scratching, saw from the corner of his eyes that it was coming again. Down it shot, wings partly closed, and Cockabundle, quick as light, shot upwards to repel the rush. In the merest fraction of time he was a yard from the ground, and his back was downwards, his strong, clawed feet towards the sky.

The sparrowhawk must have made a slight miscalculation, for I cannot believe that he really meant to meet Cockabundle that way up. But meet they did, and with a thud that could be heard two hundred yards away. The feathers flew—nor were they all pheasant feathers! Some were grey, and barred with the livery of the freebooter gentry of the wild.

The hawk screamed, but next moment he was on the ground, on his back, and Cockabundle was on the top. It was some fight while it lasted, for Cockabundle handled that hawk as a secretary bird handles a snake. But it was like fighting a bundle of barbed wire. He thumped and hammered with his feet, then, as the hawk righted himself and tried to rise, the pheasant caught him by the feathers of the neck, pinned him down, and hammered him again.

How it would have finished I do not know, for the human observer was too keen, and showed himself. Cockabundle got up and rocketed off. The hawk also got up, and flew in the opposite direction. He looked very much of a second-hand hawk, and he left three long tail feathers sticking grotesquely in the peat. And thereafter the observer maintained a real respect for Cockabundle, for a sparrowhawk, even on the ground, is no mean antagonist.

That evening the cock pheasant mounted the lichen-covered fence at the wood foot and rasped out his sunset song. It was a curious thing, that song of his, and he was no more able to resist it than are the coyotes of the ranges able to resist their twilight devotions. Every night, just on dark, he sat up and crowed and " alarmed " and cackled, till one might have thought that the whole wood was alive with pheasant, and his harsh and strident tones penetrated far, till friend and foe alike knew his whereabouts.

Yet Cockabundle's song, like the coyote's song— like all things in Wild Nature, indeed—had its special purpose. Sometimes he cut it short—as when the mist wreaths beat against the branchless limbs, and the leaves held their wild dances down the open aisles; but when it was sunny and bright he gave the countryside a special dose, flying from point to point as he warmed up to the business.

All day Cockabundle skulked and watched, and crept with head down and dropping tail, fearing his foes, but at this hour he simply *had* to let himself go, and now, having done his worst, having made the whole woods echo, he strolled into an adjacent bracken clump, and in the centre of it mounted a moss-covered boulder, so that he could see all round without being seen. It was as though he were afraid of the consequences of his own noisy work, and for once his fears were not ungrounded. For presently, as the shadows deepened, as the last of the cushats alighted with silent flight in a fir tree near, Cockabundle suddenly became uneasy.

So did the cushat, for scarcely had he arrived when he was off again, this time with a resounding clatter of wings. It meant, " Look out!"

Cockabundle looked, and saw! He saw a rounded head and two big ears rise slowly from a bunch of wild honeysuckle clinging to a windfall as the young fox looked around for the songster. Then Cockabundle rose, and flew with a terrific burr of wings clean off to the other side of the wood, crowing as he rose. Truly he had not ascertained that the side to which he was going was safe, but he had at any rate arrived at the fact that the side he was leaving was unsafe, which was a step in the right direction.

Cockabundle did not sleep on the ground, nor did he run much risk of the branch on which he slept giving way under his weight during his slumber. He chose the limb of an oak, as thick as a man's thigh and about twelve feet from the ground. He had slept here often enough before, but he had other roosting-places, and always he made his selection with due regard to wind and weather. He was an infallible weather prophet, was Cockabundle, for if dusk found him on his wet-weather seat, then assuredly it would rain before morning.

But Cockabundle had other enemies in addition to the hawk and Mr. Reynard, for that evening the farmer's boy had seen him seek his roosting-place, and the boy decided to carry into effect a poacher's wrinkle of which he had heard. About two hours after darkness he lit his acetylene cycle-lamp, and thus armed he sallied off to the foot of the tree in which Cockabundle was roosting.

The old cock pheasant moved uneasily, prepared for flight; but as the brilliant light came to rest directly beneath him, shining up into his eyes, he became strongly fascinated by the mystery and power of it. He stared and stared, while meantime the light drew nearer.

No wild creature lives to grow old unless circumstances favour it. Even in our world it has almost passed into proverb that coincidence possesses a long arm, but in the wild that arm is longer than comes within the reach of our wildest dreams. The hairbreadth escape is a daily affair, and beyond it lies the far narrower margin of chance, and chance upon chance, finer than the finest gossamer spiders spin, which, in turn, is inconceivably finer than any fabrics of man and his machines.

The desire to possess an acetylene cycle-lamp had been a long-prevailing and a long-unrealized desire in the mind of that country boy. An unexpected fortune had eventually enabled him to buy the lamp, and he treasured it as a possession aloft and aloof from his other possessions, save for the rusty cycle which unexpectedly became his when his uncle was killed by a bull.

Leaving the out-buildings that night he had, in his excitement, turned the lamp full on, in order to obtain the maximum results; but now, as he elevated it by means of his pole to the level of the pheasant, the cheap and flimsy structure refused to withstand the strain.   In short, it burst—exploded into an uproar of ruddy flame, and the boy, inheriting his father's dread of modern things which are apt to explode, fled into the darkness, his eyes dazzled, till he fell head-over-heels across the brook which marked the boundary on that side of the wood.

As for Cockabundle, he also fled.   He did not fall prostrate into the boy's arms, as per the text-book; but he exploded into flight towards the open moor, and, alighting in the heather, he spent a troubled night meandering aimlessly.   And the grouse, moreover, were aware of his presence, for he kept about two score of them awake.

It is not possible to recount Cockabundle's history day by day.   Often I saw him on the narrow road which runs through the wood, and I soon came to regard him as a past-master in the art of camouflage, as in the art which it has come to accompany.   He, if anyone, knew the value of " freezing ", knew the meaning of protective colouring.   You saw him on the road, you saw him run into the shadows of the trees; then he vanished.   Stopping at that point and searching, he would rise suddenly at your feet from a leaf-bank where there was insufficient cover to hide a mouse.   Yet Cockabundle knew that his coat

matched those leaves, and that, so long as he remained motionless, he was all but invisible to the
human eye. It was characteristic of him that always
he ran a few paces and hid till danger was past, when
he would quietly return to his interests; while the
black game and the woodcock and the roe deer fled
straight away, and wasted valuable hours of feeding-
time getting back, he got over it by hiding.

The twilight hours were Cockabundle's feeding
hours, and his life was not one of high tension—
indeed, that of few wild creatures is. He had more
relaxation than most men, and certainly a good deal
more than most women. For hours on end he would
scratch and roll and doze and peck in some favourite
sunning place, and certainly I believe that he, whose
coat partook so much of the sunshine, was not dead
to the beauty of sunlit things. There, under his peat
bank, the scent of heather in his nostrils, the warmth
of the coming spring playing upon him, he would
lie for a time, surveying his sunny surroundings;
then, as though it were all too much for him, he
would veritably sprawl and wallow in the warmth,
and with a freedom of pose which might not have
been becoming for any less elegant than he. Then,
after a while, coated with dust, Cockabundle would
hop over the high boundary wall into the wood, and
when he shook himself one saw only a floating cloud
of dust as when one steps on a giant fuzz-ball. But
the dust would drift away, and there, from the centre
of it, Cockabundle would materialize, more radiantly
beautiful than ever.

Spring assuredly was coming. And each evening

Cockabundle sang on the lichen-covered fence louder and longer than he had sung during the lean days of winter. There was an inspiration in that song. It told the other pheasants, full of all the opening promise of life which comes to the wild folk with the spring, that over there were brimming banks and shady glades. Thus, as coyote answers the sundown song of coyote, as beaver answers the castor sign of beaver, other pheasants drifted in to share Cockabundle's territory. He had called loud and long, not knowing why he called, but now the purpose of it was made evident.

Very early one morning a motor-cyclist, in even more of a hurry than most of his breed, for he knew the road and he had a good machine, rounded a bend in the road which runs through the wood, and came suddenly upon two cock pheasants fighting in the centre of it. So preoccupied were they that he was able to take stock of the situation. The whole road was littered with feathers. They sailed majestically on the still air, and clung to the sticky sheaths of the chestnut buds.

One of the pheasants looked decidedly war-worn. He was sitting down, and his head seemed to be nodding feebly. Yet, as the motor-cyclist approached, he rallied his strength and struck at the other, which ducked and ran forward, so that the spurred feet of the assailant alighted only on the fleshless tail of his target. The other spun round, and thus whisked the foothold from under his aggressor. Instantly the tables were turned, and the moth-eaten pheasant was on his back, to be pounded as Cockabundle

7

once pounded the sparrowhawk. Thus we see the value of Cockabundle's tail. It was there to deceive his foes, for it gave to his person a deceptive length, half of which was camouflage.

As the motor-cyclist came up the two birds separated. He who was obviously the loser fluttered straight up, and struggling for a winghold, flew clean across the valley and out of sight. The other, dodging the front wheel by scarcely a yard, merely ran. He refused to rise, but as he scuttled over the crisp leaves the reason for it became obvious. For, from nowhere in particular, three hen pheasants, in their demure grey, suddenly rose and ran after him. After him, I say, or rather, I should say, they chanced to take the same direction.

Cockabundle fought many battles that spring, for always he was ready to meet his own kind, and to do battle for those who were not of his own sex. But, as concerned the rest of the wild kindred, Cockabundle never fought if there were a way out. He would not fight the blackcocks nor the capers, not because he was afraid of them, but because it was against his principles. Always, excepting his own kind, he would go right away rather than try conclusions, even though the stranger were obviously weaker than he was.

There was not really much to admire in Cockabundle's matrimonial morals. He was a bombast and a braggart, and free love was the order of his villainy. Yet when the day came for a higher call he did not fall short.

Free love and many loves, faithless to each in that he was faithful to all, yet when that morning the brown-coated, white-fronted murderer came through the heather, its black-tipped tail bushed out like a bottle-brush, Cockabundle it was who flung himself at its feet, and, feigning lameness, somersaulted head over heels, leading the stoat out of the danger zone—away from one of Cockabundle's wives, cowering in the grass with her newly hatched chicks.

But the stoat was old. He had been fooled that way before, and, after following Cockabundle a few yards, he set off back along his original line of travel.

Death stared the little family in the face, but Cockabundle came back. He alighted a yard in front of the little murderer, and with head held low, wings outspread, he cried, " No road!"

There could be but one end to it, and Cockabundle must have known. There was a hissing snarl, a beating of wings, a pounding of gallant spurs against the peat; then Cockabundle rose, upward, heavily, into the dazzling light, rocketing over the pines, but, clinging to him in the grip of death, was the living death whose path he had diverted.

Up, straight up, went Cockabundle, higher than the merlin flies in its love-flight, higher than the cushat heading upwards with the dawn; towering towards the gossamer clouds, a trail of gossamer feathers marking his course, then off across the wood, on slanting pinions now, towards the lofty fir which Quask, the heron, loved. But near it, Cockabundle faltered in his flight. He staggered, checked, then, planing headlong on, he struck the topmost branches, shimmering in their sheen of brightest green. He struck, and crashed, pin-wheeling giddily downwards, and with him also fell the little living death that he had carried in his flight.

He had lived like a knight of old, but like a knight of an enlightened age he died. The roe deer in the ferns below watched them fall; and as they came to rest and neither stirred, he shook his pretty head and bounded off, barking to his mate as he crashed among the hazel wands.

Somewhere a cushat was cooing to its young. By the river down below the sand-pipers called and flew and called. A sparrowhawk sat motionless on her eyrie in the pines, pondering the beauty of the shimmering world, while at the moorland edge a hen pheasant, who had witnessed the triumph of her lord through many a desperate fray, called her chicks about her to make sure that all was well with them. She thought that soon he would return, full of swagger and bombast, yet when feeding hour came with the fragrant dusk, she and her sisters craned their necks in vain. For Cockabundle, fallen at last to a foe of his own choosing, lay with that foe among the sorrel bells, and above them a foxglove reared its memorial form, a thing to wither in the wind, which is the way of the wild—more beautiful than any man-made monument, though not so lasting.

CARBO

A rocky, wind-swept island, far out in the centre of the wind-swept loch—a blue shimmer of twisted pines, clinging to the boulders with crooked tentacles; one of those vague and rugged islands which make any sheet of water beautiful. There, in the twisted pines, a colony of cormorants had nested each spring for so long as anyone could remember. There were, in all, five cone-shaped nests among the timber, but they must have been ages old, for never more than two couples bred annually. True that one might any day see a dozen cormorants squatted about the ledges, looking like queer black monuments, some with wings outspread to the wind, others apparently dozing with their serpent necks gracefully curved. No one could call them beautiful birds, and certainly they had few friends, for the quantity of fish they killed was enormous. The gillies called them Devil Birds.

Many attempts had been made to wipe the cormorants out, but the water bailiffs had now given it up as a bad job. What was the use, anyway? They had killed scores, but others always came to fill the gaps. For the sea, only twenty miles away by water, was a source of endless supply, and so this year, as before, two pairs of adult birds returned to nest, and each pair duly produced its brace of pale, lime-coated eggs.

A COLONY OF CORMORANTS HAD NESTED

The other cormorants which used the island as a club seemed to be greatly interested in the event, and would gladly have assisted in sitting the eggs had they been allowed. In truth, these hangers-on were all young birds, that is, under three years old, or they, too, would have been busy with their own nesting affairs.

Save when they sat on their rocky island, drying their wings or watching for fish, the cormorants were either fishing, going straight there, or flying straight back. Unlike the gulls, they never indulged in needless flying stunts, and seemed to have no interest in life beyond the satisfying of their own immense appetites, and getting ready for another meal. They fed entirely on fish, and when eventually the eggs chipped and hatched, and the young cormorants began to grow, the little newcomers certainly did not want for grub. Hideous, famished little creatures they were, which on the sight of an adult bird set up a terrific squalling for food, so that the whole cormorant colony was often to be seen flying back and forth to supply their needs. The result was that far more fish was carried than the young could possibly dispose of, and ere long, fishermen, passing in their boats on the leeward side of Cormorant Island, would suddenly quicken their strokes as the breeze from the pines caught them.

Very early in the morning, before there was any light at all, the cormorants began their day, while of all the loch birds save those which fished by night, they were the last to pack up after sundown. It must, however, be admitted that for all the harm they did from the angler's point of view, they were of some value in killing off the most undesirable denizens of the deep.

Their favourite fishing waters were at the north end of the loch where the river flowed into it, and here, on either side, there were steep clay-banks, which could be seen to run downwards almost perpendicularly for many feet below the surface. These clay-banks were honeycombed—perforated all over with thousands of holes, some large, some small, created by the action of the floods and enlarged by the eels. It was, indeed, a veritable eel stronghold, and in the winter months these slippery serpents came in hundreds to hibernate there. All through the year the honeycomb was full of eels, and one had only to drop a line over the edge and one was assured of as many eels as there were baits.

Now the eel is among the angler's worst foes, for it swallows the trout and robs their spawning beds. It was believed, indeed, that one reason why the eels congregated in such numbers was because the river above was well stocked with salmon, on the eggs and young of which the freshwater serpents fed. Since, therefore, the cormorants lived largely on the eels, it was felt on all sides that they at least did something to pay their way.

Ere the young cormorants could fly they left the nest and swam out with their mother across the great blue expanse to learn their first lessons. They seemed, indeed, to require very little teaching, for almost immediately they could dive quite well, remaining below the surface an astonishing time. When below they used not only their feet, but their wings also like the penguins and many other of the pukka divers, but nevertheless they could travel at great speed, and having sighted their intended quarry they would follow every twist and turn as inexorably as a hawk. So, though their quarry was often swifter than they were, it stood no chance of escape from these feathered otters.

As the days passed with sunshine and storm one of the mother cormorants led her two chicks by easy stages up the loch, roosting when night fell among the shelves on the treacherous east shore. They, of all birds, had no fear of the peregrines which dwelt among the shelves above, for the cormorant is too big and formidable for even a peregrine to sink, and moreover, a falcon seldom strikes at a diving bird. When the cormorants swam on the surface they floated so deep that only their heads and necks were visible, and should milord in blue pass by they paid no heed to the general shudder of fear as the dabchicks and the ducks and the coots scuttled for cover. So the mother devil bird led the way to the great eel bank, and it was here that the life of one of the chicks was diverted into quite unexpected channels.

One of the gardeners who worked in the castle grounds made quite a tidy sum each year by trapping and catching eels for the English market. Always he had a dozen or so lines down on the clay banks in addition to his wire traps, and one morning, on his usual round of inspection, he noticed the head of a young cormorant rising from the surface only a few feet from the shore.

The bird was looking at him with its evil, snake-like head in his direction, but he paid little heed to it beyond clapping his hands. Then, drawing in his next line, he felt a weight at the end, and as he. hauled in the young cormorant began to lash the water with its wings, coming towards him. An eel had taken the bait and the bird had taken the eel!

It was at this juncture that the mother cormorant, hitherto unseen, rose from the surface not far off, and as Rob drew in the young cormorant, struggling, hissing, and rasping, the parent bird flew straight towards him as though to make an attack. Forty feet away she rose almost vertically, and as she passed overhead she discharged from her beak a quantity of half-digested fish. Rob ducked and dodged as the evil discharge fell, but banking, the mother cormorant came back, resorting again to her own unique method of defence. Time after time she did it, till it seemed to Rob that she was capable of carrying on for ever; then, to his consternation, he saw other cormorants flying up in response to the cries for help of the youngster on the line, and within ten seconds they, too, were doing their best to add to the general unhealthiness of the vicinity.

Luckily, however, their aim was indifferent, and since Rob was determined to take the young cormorant home, he managed to haul it in. It bit and struck at him most ferociously, and Rob treated that lightning-darting beak with some respect. It was, however, a simple matter to drop a sack over his captive then cut the line, and as the hissing and rasping subsided the other cormorants flew off, for which Rob was heartily thankful.

Now Rob had often heard that cormorants are easily trained, and can be taught to catch fish, so he intended to try the experiment. His employer was a young man, keen on sport, and ever ready to try anything new. So Carbo was made comfortable in one of the pheasant rearing-pens, where the whole staff unanimously agreed that he was quite the ugliest object they had ever seen.

One of Carbo's wings was clipped to prevent any idea of flying away, though, as a matter of fact, no such line of thought ever seemed to occur to him. Evidently the hook he had swallowed, together with two feet of line, was still safely embedded, but it takes more than that to upset the digestion of a cormorant, and Rob soon learnt that he had his work cut out to supply his pet with fish.

" Why not make the young devil fish for himself?" said the laird. " We'll take him along to the pool below the mill. Bring him, Robert."

And the laird tramped off, leaving Rob and the cormorant to bring up the rear.

It is to be feared that the laird had some time to wait at the mill ere the other two arrived—time enough, at any rate, for the miller to point out how much of his roof required repairing, and that his cowshed did not even meet the regulations. So, when eventually Rob arrived with his cormorant under his arm, his employer was in the mood to give him a rare old rating for having been so long, but was prevented from doing so by the sight of Robert's fingers, swathed in crimson bandages.

"What, did he bite you, Robert?" inquired the laird.

"Bite me, sir!" repeated the youth, staring earnestly. "He dern near swallowed me!"

In due course Carbo, with a string attached to one wing, was liberated in the deep pool below the mill, and having indulged in a good wash, he set to work to fish in real earnest. In the rapid water near the surface, shoals of tiny bleak swam, and the cormorant simply dived through them with beak wide open, inhaling them by the dozen, much as a whale inhales herring. He ate and ducked and swallowed, and presently, becoming tired of such small fry, he dived to the bottom, and presently came up with an immense eel crosswise in his bill. This, in due course, he contrived to swallow, all alive and kicking; then down he went for another and yet another, while the crowd looked on in growing amazement at his appetite.

"Och!" muttered Rob. "I understand now that the mother cormorant might have kept up her barrage for close upon a fortnight."

How many fish of one kind and another Carbo swallowed during the two hours that they watched him no one troubled to count, but when finally he came ashore it was not because he was satisfied, but because Rob hauled in the line.

"There," said the laird, "we know, at any rate, that a cormorant prefers eels to any other fish, so you can tell the water-bailiffs that they need not trouble to shoot any more of the devil birds. Probably they pay their way."

Ere long Carbo became so tame that he was released from the pheasant pen and given free run of the property; but still he seemed to regard the pheasant pen as home, and as his food was brought him regularly he seldom left that place. At daybreak he would waddle down to the burn at the foot of the keeper's garden, and there wash and splash for a few minutes, dabbing at the ducks if they passed within his reach; but the burn was so shallow that his associations with it never seemed to rouse his instinctive desire to fish. And after his ablutions he would waddle slowly back to the rearing-pen, there to sit for hours with wings extended, imagining that he was drying out his flight feathers.

Certainly Carbo did not lack the power of imagination. For instance, he would duck his head into a pheasant drinking-trough, and lying in the dry, hot grass, he would go through all the contortions of a bird washing itself in the immeasurable depths of mighty waters. He would even go so far as to raise his body in the headlong plunge for deep water, and so, having moistened little more than his crown, he would sit for hours in the most breeze-swept spot, drying out his wings by gently fanning them. But for all his foolishness there were times when Rob, who tended him daily, seemed to see a cunning twinkle in those bright eyes, as though the bird was only awaiting an opportunity of taking a rise out of someone.

One day in the early winter the laird looked up
the young gardener.

"Robert," he said, "what about an afternoon
with the cormorant? He framed well last outing,
and it's time we got him trained. There are a number
of big trout lying at the loch head. We'll go along
this afternoon and see if he can catch one or two."

So that afternoon the line was again attached to
Carbo's wing, and he was taken to his native water
front, but this time there was a difference, for about
Carbo's throat, just below his head, was knotted a
ring of cord. The ring was quite slack, permitting
him to breathe easily—no tighter, indeed, than a
dog's collar, but it was to perform a very important
purpose. For with that cord about his neck Carbo
would not be able to swallow the fish he caught.

The throat of the cormorant is quite an elastic
affair, as indeed it must be for the bird to swallow
a fish as thick as a man's wrist. So it will be seen
that quite a slack ring meets all requirements, for
any fish the bird could swallow with the ring in
place would be too small to be worthy of a place in
the catch. Thus equipped, then, Carbo was given
his freedom.

Soon he was busily at work, and every time he
appeared on the surface with a fish, which he immediately tried to swallow, he was drawn gently but
firmly ashore, and made to give it up. Having done
so, the cord ring was slipped off, and he was presented with a small herring by way of recompense.

An hour or so of this, and Carbo began to understand the business. Returning with a catch he did

not try to swallow it, but straightway swam ashore, dropped his catch, and gaped and gasped for his deserved reward. So ere the sun was down they had him well trained, while Rob, in return for his pains, had a huge basket of fat eels to send off by that night's bus. For while there were eels to be caught the bird would search for nothing else.

Next day they took Carbo out again, the laird accompanied this time by several members of his shooting-party to see the show. The line was used as before, but Carbo behaved himself so well that it seemed an entirely unnecessary precaution. Therefore the laird remarked:

"Let him free, Robert. No need for the line. He'll come back without it."

Robert looked doubtful, but like a good servant he obeyed promptly, though as he did so he thought he saw that cunning gleam come back into Carbo's eyes. When the line was loosed Carbo sedately shook himself, then quietly launched off as before. Twelve feet out, however, he looked cunningly behind him, then began to quicken his pace. He swam thirty feet or so, dived, and as they waited for him to appear they suddenly caught sight of him far out in deep water, paddling away from them for all he was worth, heading for the cormorants' island!

The boats were fetched immediately, and a small flotilla set out in pursuit of Carbo. As well might they have attempted to catch one of the wild cormorants which were flying constantly overhead, for Carbo was able to dive unbelievable distances, and rising with only his head above the surface he was still able to make good time ere someone again spotted him.

So the sun sank to her setting, and eventually the party returned home after a very merry if entirely unsuccessful hunt.

But Rob was somewhat heavy-hearted, for he thought that his cormorant with the ring about its neck was, for all it had gained in the way of freedom, destined to suffer a long and lingering death by starvation.

In this Rob was wrong. For three days Carbo remained at large, and doubtless he became acquainted with his wild brothers and sisters, but as hunger began to press, his infallible sense of direction served him well, and homewards he turned. So, on the fourth day, Carbo was found in his old accustomed place in the rearing-pen, calling very loudly for food, for which he did not need to wait too long.

Thus Carbo went up in the estimation of the household, and that winter he became a little more interesting, for he took to exploring the property. Often he wandered up to the great stone house and pecked at the long french windows for food to be given him, and such requests were never ignored. So strange and incongruous a beast was he that he at least lent something to the atmosphere of romance of that romantic old place, yet in some ways he proved anything but a desirable pet.

For example, there was in the evergreen fountain at the foot of the gentle turf undulations below the french windows a very ancient carp, supposed to be some hundreds of years of age, the last and sole survivor of a most historic race. The fish was a general friend of the household, and would take food from the hands of anyone who offered it. Carbo murdered that carp, and his way of announcing his crime was not exactly a pleasant way.

One morning, when the household was at breakfast, Carbo appeared at the window. He knocked frantically, and the while seemed to be in great distress, as though on the point of apoplexy. The laird ran out and stroked him soothingly, whereupon Carbo produced from his capacious gullet the treasured carp, complete, though it looked half boiled!

And on yet another occasion Carbo distinguished himself. It was a mild, sunny day, and the governess with the two children was sitting stitching under one of the great copper beech trees. It was a pretty picture, for accompanying the children was the house Persian with her two kittens, with which the children were playing. And Carbo, who for the last hour had sat like a monument at the edge of the gravel path, presently waddled up to lend the lustre of his presence to the family gathering.

Slowly and sedately he came, as though anxious to be one of the merry party though fearing rebuff, but no sooner had he really arrived than his head shot out, quick as the strike of a rattlesnake, and one of the kittens simply disappeared. Then, slowly and sedately, Carbo waddled back to the point from which he had come.

8

Carbo caught many fish for the household that winter, but never again was he liberated without the line. On one occasion he spent over an hour trying to haul a huge pike from the depths of a hole in the burn, becoming so exhausted that they had to draw him ashore and take him home. A day or so later the pike was washed up on a sandy ridge below the pool, lacerated from end to end by the bird's razor-edged bill. It weighed fifteen pounds.

Carbo had become so tame and was so contented with his lot that it never occurred to anyone to clip his wing a second time, and so, that spring, when a wild cormorant flew overhead above the pheasant pen, swerving in its flight as it caught sight of the earth-bound captive below, Carbo uttered a choking cry, spread his great black wings, and rose heavily into the heavens. It was the first time he had left Mother Earth, yet, as he had known how to fish, as he had known without learning how to swim and dive, so now he knew how to fly.

Very heavily he rose, but once clear of the trees he seemed to get into his glide, and so—

Farewell, old place! Farewell, Rob, and my many kind, unnatural friends! These are my horizons, vague, and vast and infinite, the unending lochs, the unending hills, and ever beyond the unending sea. My lot so far has been a strange lot, but I belong to a strange race, which man can never know. From the Devil Birds I came, and to them I now return. Farewell!

THE GREY RANGERS

I

A thousand feet above the topmost peaks, the five grey crows were flying. From earth below they appeared as the merest specks, and without the aid of glasses it would have been hard to judge their movements. A few seconds of observation, however, would have shown that there was some kind of system in their madness, for they hung about the same place, rising, falling, wheeling, and gliding, while their harsh clamour was just audible in the glen below.

They were grey crows—hoodies, or Norwegian crows, as you choose to call them, though very clearly three of the five had never been to Norway. One could pick them out from their parents by their strained and shuffling flight, and it was evident that they were measuring their powers for the first time. Nor would they have remained where they were but for the old birds, who, circling just above, were calling and encouraging, and when now and then a youngster staggered and cried, one or other of the adults would sweep down to reassure it.

But there was an additional attraction, which kept the minds of the chicks busy and held them up, for each of the parents carried something in its beak, the one a stiff flight feather, the other a piece of stick about the same length. These articles they dropped at intervals. First the feather would waft earthwards, spinning, and changing its angle as a feather does, and the young would flutter after it, trying to catch it in mid-air, and calling loudly in the heat of rivalry as, time and again, they missed. Then, to show how easy it was, an old bird would dive headlong, dip below the clamouring chicks, and catching the feather with a click, would mount heavenwards, the youngsters once more rising in pursuit, like puppies after their mother. The stick was easier, for though it fell faster, it fell straight, but when at length one of the chicks caught it, he was so hotly pursued by his brother and sister that he was glad enough to let go his prize.

When the sun dipped from view, though the heavens remained radiantly aglow, the young crows descended to their native tree, flapping and circling, while ninety or a hundred feet above their parents still wheeled; and even when the last of the chicks had shuffled awkwardly into the home pine, the old birds remained aloft, searching evidently for a possible intruder, then they closed their wings and lightly dropped.

As a matter of fact, the grey crows were not in much danger of intrusion in that quiet corner of the range, for this was deer forest. The destroying hand of the keeper played no part, and the stalkers had no quarrel with grey crows and the like—indeed, they rather welcomed the presence of the carnivorous birds, which helped to keep down the grouse and the hares and the other keen-eyed folk who often warn the deer. So the unwieldy bundle of sticks in the heart of the pine had escaped the charge of shot which would have been its lot in grouse country, but though the chicks were now strongly a-wing, they still regarded the nest as home.

But for all the homely beauty of that sundown flight, the grey crows were real blacklegs, and of this there was evidence enough the following dawn. A cold mist hissed across the mountain face, and the crows were ranging the country after the systematic manner of their kind, the old birds leading, while the chicks flew from rock to rock, guided by their call notes. Thus they were learning to hunt as they had learnt to fly, when presently the father crow alighted on a boulder and uttered a dismal croak. The mother grouse crouched lower, deadly afraid but deadly prepared, and in the space of a few seconds the crows were all round her on the rocks. Knowing now that she was discovered, the hen grouse uttered a desperate croak, and started to run towards the nearest snow-drift, sweeping her young along before her outstretched wings.

But in an instant the crows were there, buffeting her with their wiry pinions and striking viciously with their sable beaks. The young crows alighted in the heather, bristling and shaking their wings, their mouths wide open, but taking no actual part in the encounter, save that they completed the ring. Then, while one crow held the red bird's attention, the other aimed at slaying the chicks with lightning thrusts of its beak, and there, among the dripping rocks, in the cold, dim light of the cheerless dawn, there was a nice little tragedy in the making.

But things did not pan out just as the robbers had

intended, for there sounded overhead a strong burr of wings, and the cock grouse came hurtling down to join the fray. He was brave, and he knew how to use his feathered, owl-like feet. He was quick as a weasel, and bristling with fury he caused just that diversion which enabled the chicks to slip under the snow-drift, the edges of which were eaten away by the action of trickling water. So they were safe, and another burr of wings bore off their parents, like the wraiths of the mist they were.

Ten minutes later the family of grey crows might have been seen feeding on the carcass of a mountain hare in the clear atmosphere at the burn edge a thousand feet below—a hare which somehow had hit hard times; and when they had finished, there was nothing left of that hare save the capsized skin, deeply trodden into the peat hag.

Though there had been plenty of rain in the glens and sleet in the hills, that spring had been remarkable for its absence of wind, but a day or two later a tearing nor'wester swept the range as though to make up for lost time. It was a living, palpable thing, that gale, and on the same day the grey crows were seen for the first time in the glen bottom. Hitherto they had ranged little lower than their home pine, which stood at top timber level, but on the morning of the gale the postman, who was about the only human soul who used that road, came round a corner on his cycle to find three crows in the centre of the road, clearly in a great state of agitation. Almost immediately he realized what was amiss, for the crow between the other two was obviously a youngster. Its parents were on either side, debating eagerly, for the young crow, which had been swept into the sheltered hollow, sat all hunched up, evidently determined not to lose the hold on terra firma he had at last obtained.

At the man's approach the parents rose, fighting the wind, but the chick did not stir till he actually stretched out his hand to lift it, whereupon it rose with a frightened croak, instantly to be caught by the gale and borne off like a rag. Next moment it crashed headlong into the wire deer fence, and fell to earth, a crumpled mass of feathers.

That, indeed, was an anxious day for the parent crows, for it was as though Dame Nature had sent the gale to scatter wide the fledglings of the year. Another of their two remaining chicks was swept clean away, how and where they never knew. Doubtless the wind caught her when they were busy elsewhere; perhaps she was swept out to sea, or perhaps the stalker in the next glen, who saw a peregrine descend from the crags and knock down a young crow, simply because it was helpless in the wind, might have enlightened the parents. The peregrine did not want the crow, of course, but there is no love lost between the feathered hunters of the hills.

As for the third young crow—who had caught the stick in mid-air, and who now had proved the fittest—he was safe that day in the heart of a small fir planting at the roadside, and there, among the ferns and brackens, he had sense to remain till the gale had blown itself out. This one, the fittest, we shall know by the name of Cornix.

II

Cornix and his parents lived and hunted together through that summer, as the whole family would have done had they remained united. In this respect, as in many other respects, they were in common with the ravens, their near relatives who shared their environment, but the blood bond between the crows and the ravens was that of blood spilt. Often Cornix and his parents fed at dawn or dusk on the carcass of a stag or a braxy sheep along with the raven family, seven strong, born in the same corrie, and at these gatherings the crows and the ravens seemed to be on the friendliest terms. But one morning Cornix went alone to the feast, and though the ravens came with their usual profession of friendship, one of them tried to stab him in the back, and he had to flee in peril of his life. Similarly, he and his parents set about a young raven which they found bathing in a crystal stream, and they gave him a hammering he was not likely to forget for many a long week.

When the winds of autumn began to blow, a strange restlessness fell upon the crows, and with the cold bustle of the November days, Cornix and his parents were wont to rise a-wing, and sometimes they played the game with which this record opened. True that Cornix never learnt to master the gale and to mould it to his will as did the eagles, the buzzards, and the great black-backed gulls; he was always clumsy in a wind, but now that the home pine had lost its ties, the three of them, with the spirit of exploration upon them, were wont to circle down the gale, steadily eastward, over hill and valley and loch and forest, alighting to feed where the rooks or the gulls were feeding, and sometimes they soared heavenwards in the stillness of evening with those vast armies of feathered folk, which ever grew as winter came on. Food did not trouble them, for the grey crows could eat almost anything—grubs, worms, vegetable matter, carrion. They could live as the starlings lived, as the rooks lived, as the gulls lived, and they could snatch a fragment of floating food from the bosom of the racing surf as adroitly as the swiftest gull.

They learned, moreover, what the gulls already knew—that where the lapwing flocks had gathered there was insect fare, and that if one watched the lapwings they were easy to rob by dint of swift wing beat and dagger thrust. So, as they travelled eastward with the prevailing wind, the day came when the grey crows could travel no farther unless they crossed the sky on earth, which is the sea.

To Cornix it was strange, but evidently his parents knew the place, for they alighted at once upon the shore, which was littered with boulders and draped with weed. Here there were many other grey crows, and all of them seemed to know the business well. The tide was running out, and the crows were moving abreast of it—scores and scores of grey-cloaked ruffians, extending all along the sands and keeping pace with the receding tide. They hunted among the weeds, glancing into the pools, stabbing here at a stranded star-fish, snatching up a shrimp

LAPWINGS WERE EASY TO ROB

or a prawn, or anon gathering in a noisy scramble
for some stranded delicacy of greater bulk than the
finder could conceal. And Cornix, being adaptable,
fell in line, and ere the tide was fully out, he flew
back with his parents, gorged and satisfied, to preen
his feathers on a high tide sand-bank along with a
company of dapper oyster catchers.

But as dusk gathered, what was perhaps the most
mysterious chapter of the grey crows' lives turned
its opening page, for, along with his parents and
many of his kind, Cornix wheeled and circled over
a narrow glen which cut the sea cliffs clean asunder
at their highest point. It was a closed-in, desolate
little valley, which only the sunlight of dawn could
gain—a valley of stunted, twisted alders, cowering
low with knotted grasp, a valley of dead and dying
trees, stark and dim and cheerless, through the
depths of which a white torrent thundered, while
the rocky slopes rose sharply to the heights above.
It was over this washout—truly a washout—that the
grey crows hung that night, an inconceivable company of them, circling, criss-crossing, for this was
the first great gathering of the clans. Solitary at all
other times, they had now united, but not till the
sun was gone, leaving the coast in purple shadow,
did the crow army descend, led by their veteran
leader. They settled in the stark and twisted trees—
a single clump of trees deep down in the valley
gloom, and there, fluttering their wings and extending their necks, they croaked and clamoured and
carried on what might have been an unholy ritual.

I do not pretend to know the meaning of these

strange winter gatherings of the grey crows. I only
know that the oldest inhabitant along that stretch
of coast would have told you that on a certain day
in November the grey crows gather thus, and there,
night after night, that fringe of trees is grotesquely
crowded with their monk-like forms. At sunrise
they are gone, each family to its individual hunting,
but each dusk through the winter they return to
hold their strange parliaments, and perhaps to decide those things by which the crows, cursed above
other vermin birds with the blast of shot and powder,
are yet enabled to keep their hold on life.

At these gatherings Cornix had little to say. Like
other youngsters of that season, he preferred to be
apart, and only when another crow alighted alongside him, did he open his capacious beak and croak
his sepulchral contribution.

Thus daily Cornix and his parents scoured the
shore following the tide, and when hunger held the
hills, the sea brought its daily bounty, and of the
bitter pinch of winter the grey crows knew nothing.
Once, to be sure, Cornix all but lost his life. He
found a monster shellfish lying open, and he aimed
a dagger thrust to snatch out its heart, but the shellfish was in the act of closing when the blow fell, and
the vice-like grip locked on the young crow's murderous bill. So Cornix would have remained a
prisoner till the rising tide claimed him, as it has
claimed so many longshore feeders, but luckily for
him the shellfish was insecurely anchored, and he
managed to drag it up and to hammer it to bits on
the rocks.

Thus we have seen how the grey crows live, which is *why* they live—these birds hated by all where the preservation of other bird life is considered worth while. That winter was one of hunger and hardship in the hills. Even the eagles descended to the glens and paid with their blood the price of famine, but the grey crows lived in plenty by the endless bounty of the sea.

One bright and sunny day early in February, Cornix and his parents had been busy harrying three or four small brook trout up and down the tiny unfrozen pool in which the fates had stranded them, when his father suddenly set upon him, much as he and his parents set upon the young raven. I do not think his parents would have killed him, but at any rate Cornix was glad enough to quit the place, and when at dusk he got back to the washout where they had rested all winter, he found only a smattering of the original company gathered there—the young birds of last season. Like himself, all seemed a trifle ruffled and ill at ease, for all of them that day, or during the gleams of sunshine of the preceding days, had lost their parents, to whom the call of spring had come.

So for Cornix yet another phase of life opened. He became a pack hunter in the true sense—that is, he threw in his lot with any ragtime company he came across; and as spring advanced, the straggling bands of youngsters passed inland again. Cornix did not mate, though truly he had many a lively dust-up with some gay young bachelor like himself when a lady hove in view. One might have seen

these heedless gatherings of grey crows scouring the
shores of the hill lochs, the next day feeding with a
motley multitude of rooks, or basking on the mud
flats with the swarms of black-headed gulls, which
also were thronging inland. Again, in the dusk of
evening, a forester saw them gather—fifty grey
crows if one—about the branches of a mighty pine
which that day the lumbermen had felled. It seemed
that the crows were holding an indignation meeting
on man's vandalism, but when the forester found in
the topmost branches of the pine the old nest of a
crow, and was told that for many years a family had
been reared there, he thought he understood, for
he knew that the crows are a clannish lot.

Then, as food became more plentiful, the band of
youngsters split up, and by the end of May Cornix
was a solitary crow, who looked to his fellows for
nothing, and met them as strangers or as deadly
rivals. So he lived his life till November came again,
and with the falling of the leaves and the ghost dance
of the faded bracken along the pine slopes, he
turned eastward to the sea.

III

It was, of course, to the same place, with its
twisted trees and its thunder of white waters, that
Cornix returned, and there, as the dusk fell, the
mighty gathering of the clans again took place, but
Cornix no longer remained in the background.
Instead he was a leading light on a topmost branch.
Understanding had come to him, for he was among

the first to take his place beside one of his choice,
and thereafter daily he and she flew in double har-
ness. Of love-making there was none. They simply
linked arms, as it were, and through the chill blasts
and the storms and the thunder of the wintry sea,
Cornix and his mate lived and ate and had their
beings always within a few feet of one another. So
other young crows met and married in the first days
of winter, and, be it understood, they married for
life, unless some misfortune should come to sever
them.

Of such misfortune—one night a very old crow
came in to join the clans. She was alone, and she had
lost one eye, evidently through a desperate encounter
of some kind; she was wet and wretched-looking,
and clearly suffering. She alighted on a branch a
little apart from the rest, as though she preferred
to be alone—alone for the first time in all her many
winters. Nature is often merciful in her most inexorable moods—and was it by an act of mercy that
Cornix and his fellows rose and beat the old crow
to the ground and left her there with wings outspread? She had served her useful part, and could
serve her kind no longer, but did Cornix know that
it was his own mother at whose funeral he had
figured—if not as chief mourner, at any rate as
chief pall-bearer? That much I doubt.

Thus, till spring came, Cornix and his mate lived
in cool and indifferent partnership, but when one
February day, hunting the pools together, the sun
shone out with a warming glow, Cornix rose and
stabbed viciously at the young gentleman who was

fishing the pool with them—as a year ago, indeed, his own father had stabbed at him. Then, in the slanting rays of the sunbeams, one might have witnessed, there on the glistening sands, what is one of the most ungainly but at the same time one of the most graceful love dances in all wild bird life—the love display of the grey crow, resplendent in his simple yet wonderfully harmonious spring-time dress.

A few days later, two grey crows—they might have been the same two as for the past twenty years had nested there—set to work to renovate the old eyrie in the corrie far inland, high above which, two years ago, we saw the parent crows, who now were gone, teaching their young to fly.

GARR, THE BLUE JAY

Even one of his own bright-eyed kind would hardly have noticed Garr, the Blue Jay, as he left the wild entanglements of his own waste land, and from hedgerow to hedgerow, from spinney to spinney, made his way downhill towards the wide and fertile valley. Had one been able to follow Garr's movements, one might have known that he was on mischief bent, so cunningly did he go his way. He hopped from twig to twig with lightning quickness, dived into one thicket and next second popped out of another twenty feet away. He flew a few paces, popped into a hedge, and hopping, fluttering, dodging, appeared at the other end of the field—never more than twenty feet from the ground, yet such was his quickness that ten minutes at the most found him two miles away, and amidst very different surroundings from the unkempt common lands which were his home. Had you asked anyone living in that valley whether jays were common, they would probably have told you: " There are a few away back in the rank woodlands, but they rarely come down here, and we don't want them." But this was the first dawn light, mark you!

It was a very beautiful garden Garr had reached, already fragrant with flowers, under the shelter of moss-grown walls and stately beech and acacia, and since the day was now ten minutes older, a flood of bird song filled the thickets, though as yet few birds were to be seen. A scurry of jackdaws flew overhead against the dark-blue sky, but in silence; a woodpigeon high above the beeches flashed for an instant gold, and was gone on his dawn-lit way, and there was Garr, seated on a window-ledge of the mansion house, flirting his tail and peering this way and that with head awry. With a lightning movement he pecked at a wisp of hay protruding from the ivy, gave it a quick jerk then a wrench and a twist, and out came a sparrow's nest, its five eggs showering to the ground, while the parent sparrows shrieked in dismay at the sudden catastrophe. Two hops and a flutter and Garr was down on the gravel below, pecking up the contents of the broken eggs ere they had time to soak in, then he flew off towards the servants' quarters where something had attracted his keen eyes. It was a white sheet which a chambermaid had inadvertently left on the line overnight, so Garr alighted on it where it was pegged to the line, wiped his beak on it, scraped his boots on it, then cocked his head with an expression which might have meant: " Now they'll jolly well have to wash that again before the mistress sees it!"

Just then a stray sunbeam caught him, and though hitherto in the half light he might have been some kind of grotesque little feathered imp, one saw now that he was indeed a very beautiful bird, for the sunbeam lit up the wonderful red brown of his plumage, touched with black and white and the most beautiful blue, showed his distinguishing crest which he was for ever raising and lowering, a

OUT CAME A SPARROW'S NEST

twinkle in his bright eyes, which were humorously full of mischief. A bird, indeed, as wide awake and as keenly alive as any bird could be!

In a moment he was gone, a short, fluttering flight to the bird bath, which was moss covered and full of lilies. He drank, then with characteristic energy, fluttered at the shallow margin, casting high the spray, but in the middle of it someone threw open a window—a man servant of rare virtue, having regard for the hour. In an instant Garr shot into the shadows of a tree lupin, and said never a word, and it is unlike a jay to say never a word, except a jay far from home or on an early morning raid.

Garr listened, and no doubt his intent hearing told him much, for promptly he flew to a gable, dodged behind a chimney, and a second later was actually on the sill of the window which had just been opened. He peered into the gloomy room beyond— if man chose to live in such dungeons it was his own show!—then believe it or not as you will, that shy and brilliantly attired bird of the remote woodland thickets—the brilliantly attired are invariably shy, and have need to be—hopped in through the open window and on to the leather-topped desk with its polished brass paper-weights and inkpots. A paper-weight—no, too heavy! He took up an ivory knife but dropped it with a clatter, then in sudden panic dabbed at the nearest thing available—only a brass pen nib lying in the pen rack. In an instant he was out again; then the manservant re-entered, and looked round somewhat mystified. Spooks! The darn old house was full of spooks!

By that time the bright-eyed spook was back at the bird fountain, where he poked the brass nib under a ledge of concrete, then flew off, for the day was getting on. Man was already astir, and when man is astir the thickets are the only place for a jay, and the denser the thickets the better. Nor far off stood a row of broody coops, and the boy whose work it was to tend them was already whistling as he mixed the food round at the stables. Well, to the broody coops Garr went, for there was only one thing he liked better than downy chick, and this morning his luck was in, for as he alighted in an acacia near, he saw mice, mice, many mice, feeding about the wooden houses, and in a moment he was down, and quick as an owl had a young mouse in his beak. He flew back to the acacia with it, and jammed it in a crevice of the bark, then down again for another and yet another, and by the time the boy appeared across the field, there were four mice lodged in the crevices of the bark—four mice which might just as easily have been four pheasant chicks, but that the laws of compensation are for ever at work. Wild Nature always gives back with one hand what she takes with the other, though man cannot realize it.

But by now it was broad daylight, and time to bid farewell to the danger zone. Rabbits were scuttling everywhere on the dewy grass; in the centre of the avenue between the tall elms two cock pheasants were fighting hammer and tongs; woodpigeons cooed, and Garr slipped off, taking none of his spoils with him. By hedgerow and spinney he went—

back to the wild, waste woodlands on the top of the hill, and he uttered never a sound till he got there, then he began to make up for it.

Old trees, bracken, bramble and fern—a wilderness of disorder stretching far and wide, a waste land such as enables our rarer birds and beasts to hang on to existence, and here Garr's pent-up vocal engines were given release. He flew from bush to bush, chattering, bowing, and flirting his fanned-out tail, and from a thicket near a rasping came in answer. Then, in the twinkling of an eye, it seemed that all the thickets all around were alive with jays, fluttering from point to point, showing off their bright-blue wing feathers, seeking the sunnier twigs and the bush tops till the gathering made a very beautiful picture. One might have thought at first that they were disagreeing, yet there was no shade or shadow of strife—they were simply trying to outdo each other in a spirited, noisy, social gathering. For the most talkative folk are rarely really quarrelsome.

Suddenly their united rasping changed its tune to a whisper—listen! and, silently one by one, the jays dissolved, till harsh and proclaiming their telltale cry broke suddenly from another part of the wood, and one knew that the entire gathering had reassembled there. Moreover, one knew that they had now something to talk about, and so indeed had Ned Witlow the poacher, for those blessed jays had found him out! He quickened his pace through the thickets, his lurcher hard on his heels, but there behind him, in the thickets on either side, were the jays, uttering their tell-tale call. He was a fool, of course, to have taken the risk, but the more he hurried the louder shrieked and rasped the mob, yet he could not catch sight of one of them, or in his anger he might have chanced a shot.

It is an old wise saying that " those who live in glass houses should not throw stones ", but there remains the ancient truth about the laws of compensation.

That was a perfect April day and Garr and another jay, the first to appear that morning, spent the whole of it exploring the wast woodland, which they must have loved very dearly. One would have caught but an occasional glimpse of them, so closely they stuck to the thickets, yet they were a strange combination of the secretive and the self-advertising, for though they seemed ever to be hiding and watching, yet their din and chatter betrayed them everywhere. True, that when you got there they were gone, yet why for ever skulk and hide, yet for ever call out " Here I am!"

Every corner they knew, and too much about the affairs of other woodland folk, yet theirs was a fairy world among the sunlit leaves, and how delightful to hide when the sky grew dark in the woodpecker's hole, knowing that one had no right whatever there. Then when it cleared and the two flew out, Garr peered into a hedgesparrow's nest—yes, one egg to-day, and the other jay, never more than twenty feet away, flew up into a pine and came back with the daring news that the kestrel was sitting her eggs. They swore at an adder and mobbed a stoat and killed and skinned a mouse or two, and when the sun sank down there was scarcely a corner of the bad waste land they had not explored.

Now while the wild woodland seemed mainly to be abandoned to vermin, on the slopes either side the keepers were busy with their pheasant traps, by means of which the birds for the rearing-pens are caught. A pheasant trap is, of course, about as innocent and above-board as a mushroom—obvious to a jay, though any kind of a trap will do for a muddle-headed lunatic like a pheasant. By dint of a train of grain the long-tails are decoyed to their capture, but of late progress had been slow, since the jays in the wood had become wise to the proceeding, and were picking up the grain and leaving only the trap.

This evening, however, strange things were happening, for there in the open at the woodland edge was a bowl of scalded grain and raisins, and feeding from it a very fat wild woodpigeon—the wariest of birds. Assuredly the pigeon was as motionless as the ground on which he stood, yet where a woodpigeon feeds it is safe for any to follow, and down came another woodpigeon, to alight beside him, whereupon a stick with a white ball of paper at the end of it suddenly reared upright alongside the bowl, and away flew the wild woodpigeon, startled out of its wits, though the wooden one beside the bowl remained still feeding.

Then overhead circled a flight of domestic pigeons from the rectory dovecot, and they, too, were about to alight when up flew the paper wand, and away they went.

But it was becoming darker now, so—watch and listen! Not far off sounded the rasping of a jay, subdued yet beckoning, and soon a jay alighted in the grass close by, listened and looked, then hopped towards the bowl. The wand remained motionless, and down came another jay and yet another, till within three minutes half a dozen were feeding from the bowl, while at the woodland edge, ticking off the ten second intervals regular as clockwork, a jay on the watch was uttering his short, subdued rasp.

Just what happened about that food bowl one cannot quite say, for it was now about dark, but within five minutes half a dozen jays were somersaulting drunkenly hither and thither in all directions. Whether the arsenic was a little too strong or a little too weak I do not know, but at all events the jay on look-out go smelt a rat, and filled the whole night with his wild alarm notes.

" That's done it!" said one of the two men crouching in the sheep shelter near, relinquishing his hold on the string which operated the magic wand. " We shan't get no more jays after this—one of them watching to tell all the others! We'd better get out and polish them off."

But the polishing-off process was not quite so successful as it might have been, for even a very intoxicated jay takes some knocking down with a stick in the half light, and when the keeper and his friend gave up the hunt ten minutes later, every intoxicated jay had safely reached the thickets.

" Well," said Ned, " if that ain't a washout! That jay sentry seemed to be shouting orders which way to go, and they all took his word for it." And the watching jay was Garr.

Jays are hardy birds, possessed of wonderful digestions, and three mornings later two jays paid a stealthy visit to the house in the valley which, at the opening of this story, one of the two visited alone. They pulled another sparrow's nest out of the ivy—" it's the rats what does it," the gardener told her Ladyship—and they ate the little store of mice in the acacia, and bathed in the bird bath; then they flew back to their wild woodland, the sunbeams shining in their plumage, nor would they return for many weeks. For many weeks, indeed, they would be busy in their own home lives, living together, no more breathless raids or social gatherings, for though the jays know how to play, they are really home-loving birds, and very devoted to their young and the wild woodland wastes they love.

So deep in that dark thicket they built their somewhat slovenly nest, and woven into the materials of it was just one souvenir—a brass nib, stolen from a pen rack!

THE REMORSELESS RULING

The young sparrowhawks had left the nest and were now able to fend for themselves, but though no longer held together by any family bond, they still regarded the fir planting in which they had been reared as their home. It was a hidden-away little forest lying at the foot of the range, and only an occasional shepherd went that way. So any morning and evening one might have seen a whole flock of wheeling, screaming sparrowhawks about the fir spires—the two parents and their five young, and as the young grew stronger on the wing, the destruction they wrought among the wild bird life of their locality was truly appalling. There were, it must be admitted, too many hawks in that locality, and if allowed to flourish unchecked they would, ere long, spoil their own hunting by the annihilation of the wild life on which they depended.

But one curious thing was noticeable—that about the home wood of the raiders other birds were safe. Numbers of ring doves had built their scanty platforms and laid their pearl white eggs within sight of the sparrowhawks' eyrie, and all had safely reared their broods. Even now with the young hawks a-wing, several of the wild pigeons were busy with their second broods, but they went boldly back and forth under the very eyes of the hunters.

Yet, had one come to examine the eyrie of the

birds of prey, one would have found it littered with the legs of pigeons and chickens, and pigeon feathers strewed the ground below—pigeons which had been killed evidently beyond the one-mile radius of that sacred area. The why and the wherefore of this I cannot explain, but we know it is a rule among the killers to keep their thresholds clear of murder, and—listen to this!

When a hawk sets out in pursuit of its quarry it will not readily abandon the quest, sometimes becoming so fiercely intent that it will follow into the open arms of death. Yet one evening the hen hawk was seen in hot pursuit of a stock dove which was flying straight and fast across country as though with some fixed goal in view. Twice the hawk struck, and on the second impact the feathers flew. The pigeon was weakening, its fate seemed sealed, and as the bird of prey rose to strike the final blow, its fugitive swerved and headed in a desperate dive down the slope. At the foot of the slope not fifty yards distant was the fir wood, and now, true to the rules of the game, the hawk spread her tapered wings and rose vertically, abandoning the chase when success seemed certain. The pigeon had reached home. She had touched wood!

Let us follow for a while the lives of these fierce birds which hunt our forests, and we shall see how those who fear none and whom others fear live the most precarious lives of all.

In these early flights the young hawks regularly followed their parents, straggling by easy stages from tree to tree, and in this way no doubt they were shown the best hunting grounds, and were advised of the risks which accompanied each. Among these hunting grounds was the Adams Hewlitt Poultry Farm, eight miles distant from the home wood. It was a huge farm, its rearing-pens and wire screens covering an area of at least two hundred acres, and here an old man was employed to keep down the vermin. He had been a noted poacher in his day, and what he did not know by experience in the extermination of rats, crows, weasels, hawks, and the like, he seemed to know by instinct.

But the parent hawks were cunning, and many a venturesome chicken had they snatched when the old man's back was turned. Well they knew that he was their arch enemy, and on their visits to the farm they would alight first in the branches of a giant ash which overlooked the wire pens. Close at hand a woman was filling drinking-troughs from a large watering-can—she was not to be feared. A little farther away two men in brown suits were strolling with their hands in their pockets—they were the owners of the place, and to the hawks they were of no consequence. Nor was the joiner hammering down some felt roofing half a mile away, but—ah! there he goes, the old fellow with the grey coat and the cloth gaiters and the gun under his arm!

So the hawk, watching from the giant ash, would look before she leapt, and having made sure that the old man was safely out of range, there was a swish of wings, a stampede among the poultry, and much wild cackling. And the girl with the big watering-can would turn about to see a large blue hawk skimming over the wire netting, carrying a shapeless bundle in its claws. This kind of thing became of daily occurrence, and the poultry men agreed that the hawks were becoming bolder.

" You'll have to get them somehow, Tim," they told the old vermin killer. " How about fixing up a shelter and waiting for them?"

" No good, sir," announced the erstwhile poacher. " I'd wait all week, and get nothing else done. Thae hawks don't come till they see me, then they go right in at the other end of the farm."

At this Tim's employers were thoughtful. Would it be possible to disguise Tim as a female worker and to rig out someone else to represent him? On second thoughts the idea hardly seemed practical, for surely even a hawk would spot the disguise— Tim with his short, bow legs, his immense width, and his square bulldog chin covered with ginger stubble—no, not even a hawk would be deceived into mistaking Tim for a lady.

" I'll tell you what," said one of the proprietors eventually. " Come along to-morrow morning, Tim, in your blue Sunday suit. Set to work repairing the roof of the Ancona pen and keep your gun handy. While you are at it I will stroll about the other end in your old grey overcoat and carrying a gun."

So Tim went away chuckling his approval, and next morning the cunning ruse was carried into practice.

Man's brain is bound to triumph over the Wild Folk when he sets himself that task, and old Tim in his Sunday suit was busy hammering nails into the roof of the Ancona house, when out of the corner of his eye he saw some bird alight swiftly in the branches of the giant ash only eighty yards away. He glanced at his gun lying handy under a plank, and he went on whistling and hammering. At that moment a figure appeared from a hen house half a mile away—a figure wearing a famous grey overcoat, which hardly seemed to fit, and carrying a gun.

Down came the hawk, and old Tim turned. His hands were steady and his eyes were clear. The gun spoke once, and an unshapely bundle of feathers bounced and somersaulted all amongst the startled fowls.

" It's only a young bird," Tim told his employers. " Just about clear of the nest, and that's all. But I'll tell you what, sir. If that big old ash were felled we should be less troubled with the hawks. It's an old tree anyway, and it's time it came down."

So the big ash was cut, and from that day on the hawks were never again known to visit the poultry farm.

Within a mile of the fir planting a tiny village nestled at the river-side. At one end of the village, deserted and alone, stood a square stone building which had once been the schoolhouse. But for some reason it had been abandoned for that purpose, and now the local seat of learning was a wretched tin shanty at the opposite end of the " town ".

Sadly neglected, the old schoolhouse had fallen

into disrepair. For years its windows had been glassless, staring with blank, unseeing eyes across the laughter of the river, and the starlings had come to regard the deserted building as sacred to their possession.

But recently the big estate had changed hands, and the new laird was an enterprising man who realized that if he were to keep the best of his young people about him, he must improve the conditions of living. Why were the cities claiming so many? Was it because life at home was not worth while? Well, perhaps under the old regime—a niggardly and indifferent landlord, a disreputable, tumble-down old village, farms worked by obsolete methods, pasture lands sinking into swamp—life at home *did* hold few prospects, but the new laird would alter all that.

For a time the joiners and builders had been busy, and now at last they attacked the old schoolhouse, which was to be converted into a concert hall. Re-floored and reroofed, it would serve well in the direction of making life at home more attractive.

One of the young hawks was accustomed to visiting the village in the dusk of evening, and skimming low from garden to garden, darting now round the corner of a building or diving from the shadows of one of the giant elms, it was seldom he returned to the planting without a song thrush or a blackbird or perhaps even a wary starling dangling limply in his claws. The stone-breaker announced that he had seen a bird fly in at one of the glassless windows of the schoolhouse to snatch a starling from the rafters, and depart hastily from the opposite window with a screaming mob at his heels.

Be that as it may, within forty-eight hours of the old hall being renovated one of the new window-panes was found shattered to fragments. At first it was thought to be the work of some mischievous urchin, but on further examination a dead sparrowhawk was found inside the building, its slender body traversed by a bayonet of glass.

"Only a young bird," said the finder, "possibly just clear of the nest, and I guess it won't happen again."

He guessed rightly, for in this way a tradition of the Wild was broken—a tradition which said that those windows were glassless.

It is during the first few weeks of their existence, while they are yet wanting in experience, that Nature exacts the most remorseless toll upon her children. Each day finds them a little wiser, each day teaches some new lesson, and those who live to see the dawning of winter are well on the high-road to survival.

So far only eight days had elapsed since the young hawks became able to feed themselves, and two of the five were already gone. The third met his fate on the tenth morning, and once more there was an eyewitness.

Just below the village the river narrowed between the hardwood forests, taking a downward plunge through the bluebell slopes, and across the white cataract was a cable bridge, slung from four stone pillars and affording a bridle way to the grey stone mansion on the slope above. In the centre of the bridge was an iron gate which could be locked, and about the gate, to prevent people climbing round it, was a wicked *cheval de frise* of long iron spikes.

One evening an angler sat at the water's edge, watching the swifts wheeling and screaming up and down above the rapids, when a sparrowhawk flashed into view and proceeded forthwith to pursue the " devil screamers ". That hawk could fly to some tune, but so could the swifts, and for five minutes or more a dozen of them kept him busy, crossing and criss-crossing, while the hawk, screaming angrily, strove in vain to separate one from the rest. Time after time he dived like a ray of light into the thick of the little pack, but with screams of defiance the swifts would scatter, and every time he missed—just missed!

At these repeated failures the young hawk became more and more furious. Several times he almost dashed into the river, several times only a mighty wrench from the line of travel saved him from collision with the branches. Finally he shot skywards from a dizzy stoop, his pinion feathers singing in the still evening air, and then in the twinkling of an eye the angler heard a metallic thud, and the hawk, with drooping wings, hung poised against the cloudless sky.

At first the angler did not realize what had happened. The whole performance had been so meteoric that his mind had been unable to keep pace with it. But at length he rose to his feet, muttering, " Well, I'm blessed!" then he set out to cross the cable bridge.

Reaching the iron gate he took the dead hawk in his hands and tried to dislodge it, but it was so firmly wedged that he could not do so. Two of the iron spikes had passed through its body, and such was the force of the impact that one of the spikes had bent, and jammed against the next, thus holding the hawk in a vice-like grip.

" A young bird!" was the angler's summing up. " Had he lived another month or so he would have realized the folly of chasing swifts!"

Two little nigger boys—and yet another week and there was only one. A shepherd returning from the hill by the long white road which follows the burn, till that merry personality is swallowed up in the fir wood, when the road mounts steeply over the brae—a shepherd returning rather wearily from his long day's tramp, witnessed the fall of the fourth, though he played no part in it.

He noticed a number of jackdaws feeding down the centre of the road constantly ahead of him. As he trudged on the nearest would rise and alight behind him, and so he learnt that a migration of caterpillars, moving from the forests on one side to the rough pasture lands on the other, was the attraction which drew them. Becoming interested, he watched the flotilla rise and fall till he was surprised to see a hawk swoop down at one of the birds. Now, of all birds of the woods and the hills, the jackdaw is well able to guard its own interests, and as the hawk descended the jackdaw turned, belly upwards, to parry the thrust. The feathers flew, but there were as many grey feathers as black ones, and promptly both birds fell into the centre of the road, their claws interlocked. There they proceeded to fight it out, the jackdaw parrying frenziedly with his sable bill, the hawk striving to pin down its quarry and to hold it helpless.

Now it happened that the shepherd's dog was running a hundred yards ahead of him, as sheep dogs do when home and supper-time are near, and seeing the general scuffle in the centre of the road, the dog charged. The hawk saw him coming, and strove to disengage itself, but the jackdaw was too frenziedly busy to notice anything at all, and clung desperately to its opponent. So the dog caught them up, but his fangs closed only on the body of the hawk, and next moment the jackdaw was mounting on eager shuffling flight.

" You've settled him, anyway!" said the shepherd, as the dog brought the dead bird to his feet. " Serves him right for being such a dern fool as to interfere with jackdaws."

Thus within five weeks of their leaving the nest, the brood of five sparrowhawks was reduced to one. Three had perished by Dame Nature's chosen ways, and only one at the hands of man, for the keeper, like everything else about that estate when the new laird came, was old and beyond his work. Had he been young and active the hawks would probably have died by shot and powder, but even so the keeper would merely have achieved a task which, had it been neglected by him, would have fallen to wiser hands. For Nature is ever striving to retain her balance, to keep an even keel. She does not allow the strong to triumph nor the weak to multiply beyond the limits of economy. Her rules are the simplest of all rules, their working is infallible.

They were made without man's aid, and without man's aid they attain their ends. No species is allowed to prosper as the death-sum of another, and left to herself Nature does her own killing. So it is only when man demands an unnatural order, the superabundance of one and the exclusion of another, that he must take the matter into his own hands, and run counter to a ruling wiser than his own.

All that winter three sparrowhawks hunted the

fir planting, and next spring the sole surviving chick, a wise hawk now, brought his bride to nest within a few score feet of the tree in which he himself was reared. Thus there were two hawks' nests in the planting, but by then the old keeper had gone his way and a new man had come, so another story begins where this one ends.

SHUFFLEWING

Night had already fallen on the pine and bracken slopes as the many-wintered leader of the rook colony led his clanging followers home—night below, but overhead the sky was still aglow. So far gone was the light that one would hardly have seen the rooks, though one might have heard the swish-swish of their wings, and the occasional " chipping " of the jackdaw clan, which, though accompanying the rooks, were a people to themselves. They flew in a little compact wedge at the tail-end of the rook army, and they, too, had their leader—Shufflewing. He it was who repeatedly uttered the little chattering call-note, as though to keep his clan together, and thus, across the deer forest they passed, so low that they had to swerve about the pine ridges, then down into the little sheltered valley, which was a valley of old trees, where the living stand proudly among the fallen hulks of their fellows; and here, at a signal from Shufflewing, the jackdaws left the rooks, and with much calling and wing-beating, alighted among the branches of an old plane, while the rooks went on to the fir planting across the valley.

That old plane was a jackdaws' paradise of nooks and hollows, and evidently these late arrivals knew its every corner, for there followed an angry screech-ing and chattering, and a grey squirrel scrambled sleepily along a branch and whisked into another

cranny, while a band of starlings flew off, expostu-
lating wildly, to find shelter elsewhere. So Shufflewing, the jackdaw leader, saw his company safely
housed, then he sought the hollow trunk and perched
himself alongside his mate, his Best-Beloved, for
though it was autumn and their children were gone,
the company consisted of so many mated couples.
They were, indeed, all old birds, well able to guard
their own interests, and elsewhere one might have
found the discordant rag-tag packs of jackdaw
youngsters, generally some hundreds strong, scaveng-
ing the slopes with the rooks by day, and roosting
where they could find shelter. These young jackdaws were, indeed, quite a different people from the
smaller parties of adults, which had and held the
favourite jackdaw trees and cliffs, and lived their
lives as Shufflewing and his clan lived, by ways less
likely to keep good faith with man.

It was black as pitch in the hollow interior of the
ancient plane, but, had one been able to see, it would
have presented a strange spectacle. All up and down
were little jagged points and ledges, littered with
chips and dust, and the signs of bird frequency, and
above and below the grey-eyed jackdaws sat, some
squeezed into corners which they exactly fitted,
others shoulder to shoulder—all in pairs, all packed
in as though the place had been made to measure
for each and every one. They were like a company
of old monks in their mediæval tower, a grey-
headed, strangely unbirdlike gathering, and one
might have thought they were not birds at all, but
a company of strange little people, who soon might

burst forth into some weird ceremony which could have no counterpart in the world we know. At any rate, they were warm and snug, and this was the first night of frost, which was why Shufflewing had left the rooks to roost where they willed. He knew.

For all the sparkling tranquillity of the night, it was far from silent outside, for other clans were drifting down into the valley of old trees—down from the bracken slopes by the stony pathways, the red deer, who always descend at dusk. Here, too, each clan had its ruler, the master stag, who coughed and roared as he marshalled his hinds, till on every side the very bracken shook. By the time the moon was up, the valley bottom was a seething turmoil of moving shadows and monstrous sounds, and once an old stag, luckless in love, came over to vent his anger on the ancient plane, goring it and pawing at it with grotesque energy, till its hollow walls quaked under the boom and the biff and the scrape of his antlers.

To this, however, the jackdaws paid no heed, though had a passing forester so much as tapped the trunk with his stick, he would have sent them clamouring skywards. Before dawn the deer sought the stony pathways, leaving the little valley trampled black, with here and there a broken antler lying, and the coming of the silence was evidently the signal for the jackdaws to awake. Shufflewing got up and went out—how keen and grey it was!—perching himself on a branch with feathers puffed out, and there he proceeded to tick off the seconds with his sharp " chip-cock-chip ". It was the réveillé of the cold October morning, for now other bird sounds followed, though no bird was visible. This was the " flat spot ", the zero hour of the wild folk, for the creatures of the night were gone, and the creatures of the sun had not yet taken the field.

The jackdaws were in no hurry that morning, for the sun rose, and still Shufflewing sat, his wife beside him now, enjoying the pale sunbeams, preening their feathers, sharpening their beaks, but Shufflewing's clan was busy. They were busy about the hollow tree and about its hollow branches, giving the place a good old autumn clean, tearing off rotten chunks, scattering the dust, scraping and enlarging and making new nooks and crevices. The frost had reminded them that winter was not far off, had set the storage fever simmering in their minds, or perhaps Shufflewing had passed the word—" this is to be our winter home. Get it ready."

So he and his wife did sentry-go, while the others worked, but there was one who would not work— Scraggytail by name—who hopped from place to place, prying evil-eyed into the affairs of others, and causing constant strife. Every jackdaw colony has its idler, its thief, ragged in looks through constant strife with its fellows, and Scraggytail was old, bad, and, I believe, partly blind. Some day the others would unite to turn her out, or even to destroy her.

So through that forenoon the jackdaws worked, and the sun was beyond its zenith when at length they sallied forth, a solitary little band, shuffling through the air just clear of the tree tops, and, led by Shufflewing, who knew the seasons and the harvests, they went to the walnut grove by the big mansion house away down the valley, and till the sun set, they flew back and forth, garnering the walnuts in the hollow tree. The sun was nearly gone when Shufflewing and his mate, flying as usual a few yards apart, saw one of the big packs of young jackdaws busy with something high up on the slope above. They flew off to see what all the excitement was about, and there, under the pines, lay a big stag who had fought his last battle and lost, for behind his foreleg was a dark stain, signifying the upward dagger thrust of a victorious rival. The young jackdaws were feeding on him, and Shufflewing and his mate flew down to share the feast, but were roughly driven out and forced to make off. So they summoned their clansmen, and ten minutes later thirty old jackdaws held the feast against the united efforts of their children, and after much scuffling and cursing, the flock of youngsters, perhaps a hundred strong, flew off to roost, for it was now near dark.

So it was again late ere our hero led his party home, and now indeed there was a battle royal, for they found the band of youngsters in possession of the old tree, filling the trunk cram-jam full, having made themselves comfy for the night. So till midnight, breaking in on the roaring of the stags, the barking of the hinds, and the dry crash of rival antlers, the chipping of jackdaws rang from the hollow plane, accompanied by the beating of wings. Several times a pair of jackdaws would fall inter-

SHUFFLEWING AND HIS MATE FLEW DOWN TO SHARE THE FEAST

locked from the branches to finish the fight among
the bracken, and morning was not far off when the
last of the youngsters was thrown, neck and crop,
from the stronghold which Shufflewing's clan had
claimed. When daylight came, the ground below
was strewn with sooty feathers.

Nevertheless, Shufflewing and the rest were off
before the light, but they did not immediately settle
upon the dead stag, for that is not the way of jackdaws. They alighted in the pine-trees near, waiting
their turn, while in the grey dimness below a family
of ravens, seven in number, feasted upon the stag.
There was no sound astir as yet, save the guttural
conversation of the mighty crows, and presently
they flew silently off, rising simultaneously. A
moment later a grey fox appeared from nowhere,
and began to tear savagely at the carcass; but for
some reason he was ill at ease, and in a minute he,
too, was gone. Scarcely was he gone when there
followed a flurry of wings, and down came a band
of grey crows, who are the gangsters of the bird
world. So the jackdaws still waited and watched till
the crows were gone. Then Shufflewing uttered a
single " chipp ", and down they all flew, to feast
against time, for something seemed to say that this
was not a healthy place.

For five minutes they were undisturbed; then
suddenly they all flew off, apparently without reason
—all save one, and that one was Scraggytail. Quick
as light, she took hiding under the dead stag, and
there she remained, huddled till the danger should
pass, when she would rise and feast in undisturbed

possession ere the others could return. That trick
might have served the old jackdaw many times, but
it was not to work to-day, for the man carrying his
gun came steadily up and stood over the stag, already
half-devoured by those many scavengers which
every deer forest gathers. He chanced to trip over
one of the rigid legs, and from under it flew a jackdaw, crying loudly in alarm, for she knew her
dreadful peril. The keeper threw up his gun, one
shot rang out, and Shufflewing and his clan in the
pine-tree near saw Scraggytail fall, and knew, as
they had always known, that such was the inevitable
penalty of falling foul of man. Thereafter they did
not return to the feast, which was perhaps just as
well, for that evening a grey crow lay beside the
dead stag, its wings outspread, its crumpled legs
fast between the jaws of the vermin trap.

Every one has their black-letter days, and that
golden autumn morning was to prove a black-letter
day for Shufflewing. Having witnessed—and, I fear,
without a pang—the fate of poor Scraggytail, they
all flew off to the walnut grove to continue their
garnering, and Shufflewing and his mate would
have fared better had they stuck to nutting. But
Shufflewing, flying by, chanced to notice the white
dovecote standing in the old-world garden, and
there was no one about. An old jackdaw is up to
just about every trick on earth. He knows everything, and can eat almost anything, and the sight
of the dovecote reminded Shufflewing of a trick
worth while. So he rallied his clansmen, and down

they all swooped with a scuffle of wings and a loud
" chip-chip " on the white-walled dwelling of the
peaceful doves.

It was truly a *coup de main*, for in the twinkling of
an eye the jackdaws were inside the dovecote and
outside it, scattering its terrified occupants, who
knew that they stood no chance against those hawk-
clawed, sabre-billed ruffians. But it all led to nothing, since for once in a way the dovecote contained
neither eggs nor chicks, though certainly there were
indications that one of the doves had been thinking
about nesting. She had carried a long, straggling
end of raffia, found evidently in the garden, into the
cote, and as bad luck would have it, Shufflewing's
mate got her claws tied up in the raffia, and eventually flew off with it trailing behind her.

So the bad luck began, for five minutes later
Shufflewing saw his mate hanging head downwards
from a branch of the home plane, flapping wildly
and making no end of a fuss. This was a new amuse-
ment, but soon she managed to regain the branch;
but, alas, on the other side from the side at which
she had fallen, so giving the trailing strand another
half-hitch about the branch. Two minutes later she
was hanging head down again, but again she got up;
and *she*, at any rate, knew what was amiss, for she
began savagely to tear at the raffia entwined about her
toes. She managed to sever the main strand by which
she had hung, but the other strands were tightly
knotted, and she could not rid her feet of them.

All might have gone well but for the frost, and
next day Shufflewing's mate was not only hobbled,

but also lame—so lame that she could not perch properly, and fell several times. The tightly-drawn strands had stopped the circulation, and with both feet frost-bitten her chances of survival, with winter near at hand, seemed small, for the jackdaws are among those wild birds which depend very largely upon their feet.

Thus her fellow-colonists rose, according to the inexorable law of the wild, to drive out or to slay the unfit, the one which can no longer keep pace with the rest. It is a just and a good law in a world where one law only prevails—to live my life by the laws and customs of my kind, and then to sink, unseen, unsought, among the ferns; and to Shufflewing now came the choice—my life and my people, or my mate?

How long a wild jackdaw lives I do not know, but probably Shufflewing had seen his full twenty winters, and his mate, since she, too, was wise among her kind, was probably his first mate. That noon there was a living, struggling heap of daws under the plane, and from it the one whose feet were entangled eventually rose, to go shuffling off, with staggering, lop-sided flight, towards the high country. Even as she fled, the others mobbed her; but Shufflewing, flying with the rest, struck at the one who led the band, and that one fell, spinning as it strove to catch the air, and sat at length under a fallen pine which bridged the rocky gulch from bank to bank. So one knew why Shufflewing had become their leader, for he struck but once.

Thus Shufflewing and his mate went their way

alone, on and up towards the rocky heights from which the antlered warriors came at dusk—Shufflewing, who had made his choice, flying, as for many winters past, beside his mate. He had, at any rate, lived his life—lived long enough to know those tricks which bring upon his kind the curse of shot and powder. He, be it admitted, was a rogue, and though life to him was still a very lovely thing, there comes in the destinies of all a time when the hourhand wavers, and rarely does the clock resume its normal beat. In the Wild there is no sadness attached to this. It is merely the normal order of come and go, for we must not regard death among the Wild Folk as we regard it in the world we know so well.

Not far did the two fly, for Shufflewing's mate wearied and went slanting down, to alight at length in a stony little washout already hidden from the sun. Thereafter she did not try to rise.

Away where the sun lay hung a dense black cloud, casting night upon the land ere night was due, and in the chill and stagnant air there hung the scent of snow. Shufflewing's mate had fallen, I say, and now she sat there, hunched and listless, for it is thus, in cool indifference, that the Wild Folk await their turn; and Shufflewing, wheeling above, watching, no doubt understanding, began to soar—up, up, as a solitary jackdaw rarely soars.

The why and the wherefore of it I do not pretend to know, but one may witness these strange bird flights before the coming of great storms. Circling, rising, as he might have risen when he first met his lady-love in the frosty sunset of a bygone spring,

11

as though to convince her of his mastery of the air—so now he rose above his mate, to make her understand, perhaps, that he, at any rate, still had the infinite heavens at his bidding. So there they were, the one fallen for all time, the other rising—up, up, till the shadows of the earth were far below, and he twinkled as he flew among the sunbeams.

Only a wheeling speck now, like some glorious master of the air he hung—Shufflewing, of that prying, materialistic race which knows the tricks and knows the ways by which the weakness of the rest can be put to use—Shufflewing, the leader of the jackdaw clan, hung in the heavens like a flake of golden confetti, soaring falcon-like and defiant across the very brow of winter. Then suddenly he staggered in his flight, and earthward he came, down, down from light to shadow, then——[1]

He smote the earth beside his mate, smote and rebounded, a shattered pulp, and now, upon the train of feathers which marked his fall, little crystals of snow began to gather in the gloom. There was a hiss and a chill blast, and gone, too, were the gulls from the sky, though where they were gone I know not, save that they had fled before the storm. His mate shifted her footing, looked at him with that strangely wise look by which the jackdaws seem a people to themselves, then shrugged her shoulders as the storm about them gathered.

So the snow hissed and the winds blew, and the season had come against which the wise garner their grain.

---

[1] Death, due to old age presumably, comes to a large number of birds during these flights; evidently heart failure.

KLIX, THE NIGHT HUNTER

The two boys found the brown owl's nest in a hole in the ancient beech twelve feet up from the ground, and reaching in they were just able to touch the single fluffy chick it contained. So they took the owlet home, rigged up a perch for it in the gloom of the hayloft above the stables, and proceeded to feed it on waste scraps of meat.

Young tawny owls, unlike the barn variety, are not difficult to rear, and this one would gulp down practically anything thrust into his capacious maw. When being fed he would assume a most pugnacious and threatening attitude, sitting back and uttering a loud " klicking " noise. From this strange habit, shared by the young of the ring dove and a few other birds, he came to be alluded to, for want of a better handle, as " Klix ".

On the second morning, when the boys went in expecting to find the young owl ravenous, they were surprised to discover him moping and fed up, refusing to accept such morsels as yesterday he had gulped so readily. At first they thought he was going to die, then they located the tail feathers of a blackbird and presently the head of a water vole lying in the hay near to the young owl's perch. As to how the remains came to be there was a mystery, for there was no possible way visible by which any creature larger than a rat could gain access to the loft. Presently, however, a hole, the size of a rabbit hole, was found running down into the hay, and near to it a brown owl's feather, and removing the hay they found a ventilator, consisting simply of a missing brick in the wall, through which the parent owls had evidently entered to feed their chick, forcing their way upwards through the hay which covered the floor to a depth of perhaps four feet.

This, at any rate, showed why the young owl did not want his breakfast, but a more profound mystery remained. How had the parent owls located him? The wood of his birth was fully a mile and a half away. It hardly seems possible that they could have heard his feeble whimpers across that distance, but— how else could they have tracked him down?

Thereafter the adult birds came every night to feed their chick, and he needed no further support from his human captors. Each night the old birds could be heard hunting the shrubberies for their prey, or hooting and screeching dismally as they sat on the stable roof, and as the chick grew stronger and his demands upon them more persistent, they took to coming down from the wood while daylight still lasted, remaining about the steading till the sun was up. And meantime the remains found each morning in the loft told a woeful story of the massacre of song birds, for no matter what the fare of the comparatively harmless barn owl, there is no getting away from the fact that brown or tawny owls feed their young chiefly on small birds.

One morning, when the boys went in, Klix was

missing, and a search eventually revealed him sitting high up in a dead ash forty or fifty yards from the stable. So far there had been nothing in his daytime habits which suggested that he possessed any ideas of flight, but the owl of the dark hours is a very different matter from the owl of the daylight.

Had the young owl's captors been able to see him when darkness again settled they would not, indeed, have been able to recognize their pet. Where now the moping, dreamy philosopher of which our poets talk, and what of his parents? They were more like a family of feathered wild cats than anything else, and the two parent owls on their arrival proceeded to celebrate the freedom of their chick by the strangest of antics. They hopped grotesquely from branch to branch, trailing their wings, hissing, and glaring from side to side with their big luminous eyes. They wafted hither and thither, striking at each other and moaning, while anon Klix kept up a bubbling screech, fluttering from perch to perch, and more than once almost falling from the branches. Finally, the father bird flew to a neighbouring elm, and in the topmost branches he sat and hooted long and dismally, while the hen bird flew off to harry the bushes and to hunt the rickyard.

Long before daybreak came the two parent owls, coaxing Klix to follow, set off for the home wood. The journey was a circuitous one, for since Klix could fly only a few yards at a time, they were compelled to follow the tree-dotted boundary, then a hedge, then a moss-covered fence leading

steeply up the slope.   They adopted the most
effective means of getting the fledgling along, for
each of the parents carried food, one a sparrow, the
other a mole, and each straggling flight Klix made
found one or both alighted at the next convenient
perch.   So Klix was really following the food, not
his parents.

On gaining the fence, however, with the wood
only ninety yards distant, the owlet gave it up, and
alighting on a post he refused to budge another yard.
He was tired and sleepy, and he gave his parents
clearly to understand that he had experienced
enough of this wild-goose chase.   They pleaded, they
encouraged, they cuffed him.   He cuffed them back
and sat tight.   So the sunrise caught him, conspicuous from afar, and his parents were compelled to
seek their shadowy habitat, leaving him there.

The only occupants of that field were a young foal
and its mother.   The foal saw the young owl, and was
consumed with curiosity.   Several times he tried to
screw up his nerve to sniff it, but each time his
courage failed and he went scampering off.   At
length, however, he did get in a sniff, whereupon a
silent shadow descended from the air and dealt him
a sharp blow between the ears.   The claws of
the parent owl actually drew blood, so one can
imagine what effect the adventure had on that young
hopeful as he galloped off, kicking and squealing.
Thus, though they had apparently deserted him, the
parent owls were keeping good watch over their chick
from the wood.

The perilous day passed with no further adven-

THE FOAL WAS CONSUMED WITH CURIOSITY

ture, and that night young Klix really began his life as a wild owl of the woods.

In a very short time Klix was in no way dependent upon his parents, and they were busy with another fluffy chick, but, as is the way with many birds of prey, he did not forsake them, nor they him. He made his home, indeed, high up in the old beech which had first afforded him shelter, and there, in a hollow of one of the main forks, comfortably screened by the green leaves which shut out the glare of the sun, he would sleep away the daylight hours. Sometimes a wren, nosing about in search of trouble, as wrens do, would locate him, and very soon the little tell-tale would succeed in gathering a host of chaffinches, a woodlark or two, and often a stormcock or a blackbird, all chattering angrily at this deadly foe, while Klix never stirred, save that now and then he would half open one eye to look at them. They, at any rate, knew Klix and his kind as the feathered cats of the night, and so by their angry bedlam, they would have betrayed him to his own foes had there been any to heed.

Klix possessed naturally a keen hunting instinct, and he did not need his parents to tell him where to go or for what to look. As darkness settled he would waft off to the wood edge, where there was a deep washout overgrown with silver birch and white poplar. The action of the stream had undermined the steep shale banks, and the trailing, fibrous roots of the timbers now hung like giant whiskers all along the lips, a harbourage for furtive wild folk at the sun's setting. But many came to forsake it, for

soon after darkness each night Klix would come
wafting down on his silent, ghostly wings, dodging
the branches like a woodcock, and tense for the
faintest sound to betray the whereabouts of his
cowering prey. And, once having located a victim,
he would become a carnate fiend, striking deep into
the roots with his cruel claws, hissing and screeching, till the nerves of the cowering one failed, and
it fled for fresh shelter, and—died!

Thence to the dense fir wood, the domain of their
still stranger kindred, the secretive long-eared owls,
whose cat-like mewings Klix so often heard, and
there, among the deeply matted twigs, more than
one goldfinch and more than one ring-dove chick
on its precarious platform met their silent fates.

The young owl's sense of hearing was marvellous,
and having regard for this, some of the mystery of
how his parents found him in the loft may be
cleared. For Klix, wafting across the meadow,
could hear the movements of a mouse deep in the
grass roots, hear it so distinctly that he would turn
in his flight and fix his claws unerringly over the
tuft which harboured the morsel. Often, too, ere
he set out on his night's hunting, he would sit and
listen, guided by the minutest sounds—the twittering
of small birds in the ivy, the squeaking of rodents—
as to the direction he should take.

Perhaps the rickyard of the homestead down the
slope was the young owl's happiest hunting ground,
and there we see him at his best—or rather, his
worst. Incidentally, it marked the extreme limit of
his hunting range, for like his parents he recognized

a definite boundary, spending his nights within a two-mile radius of the home beech. Often now he helped to feed his younger brother, and whatever the owls were in their public lives, their home circle was certainly beyond reproach.

Sparrows roosted by the thousand in the rick-yard, and Klix soon learnt how to deal with them. He would hurl himself at the face of a rick, eyes flaming, uttering ever a snake-like hiss, and so, banging from point to point like a mad cat, he would very soon succeed in setting the whole sparrow populace astir. Scared by their foe and baffled by the darkness, they would collide with all manner of obstacles in their flight—even with Klix himself. Truly Klix was an unholy nightmare of a bird so far as the smaller feathered kindred were concerned.

One night there was a great stir among the owls of that range. The brown owls and the barn owls called their families about them with much hooting and screeching, the long-eared owls assembled in a veritable flock, all bowing and scraping and mewing, about the branches of a giant larch, which seemed to be the House of Commons of their kind. Then over the sparkling tree tops they flew, over the misty meadows where the rabbits swarmed, to the river, shining out amidst its dark upland settings.

Rain had fallen heavily, and with the coming of darkness a strange silence had settled upon the valley. No doubt it was this silence which conveyed the tidings to the owls, for it was the silence of mighty waters. To-night the river, normally babbling and gushing among its thousand thousand moss-covered stones, was sweeping brim full and in a level flood. Placing one's ear to the ground one could have heard the rumble of boulders as the very bed crept and silted, but whatever forces were at work below, only an unbroken hiss reached the ears above. Thus the water-voles were flooded out!

Yes, the water-vole thousands were to-night homeless refugees! Hither and thither they swam, battling with the current, hiding under the willow bushes which, swinging and straining, were themselves the sport of the current. For two years there had been no great spates, and the rodents, relieved of their deadliest foe, for it was the foe which hurled them on the mercy of the merciless, had increased enormously. Now their burrows perforated the river banks for miles, they possessed the water's edge in a veritable plague, and as disease comes to level up other races of the Wild, so to-night Nature was at work retaining her balance among the water-vole hordes which she had favoured too long.

If such a thing as memory is possessed by our wild birds, Klix and his friends must have remembered that night as a great night—a night of heedless, rampant murder running riot from dusk till dawn. They killed purely for the sake of killing, for that, too, is Nature's law when killing is so easy. They whipped their prey from the coloured waters, while all around ghostly shapes rose and sank again. They fed as swallows feed during a May Fly hatch, and snatching an epicurean meal they returned to kill. More than once Klix alighted, seagull-like, on the surface, and keeping his wings erect and dry would float a dozen paces ere, flapping lightly, he would rise again into the night. Meanwhile the silent stars shone out, neither approving nor disapproving, while along the banks the stoat packs ran and the adders struck, recoiled, and struck at the moving shadows in the grass.

Thus Klix acquired the habit of river hunting, and thereafter hardly a night passed but that he swept a stretch of the river on his round. It was August now, and the big fish sought the shallow waters with the rising of the moon, fighting their way over the gravel beds in pursuit of the minnows. Klix tackled his first trout simply because it was alive and moving, and though it cost him a wetting he succeeded in dragging it out among the rocks. And he found that fish was a very appetizing change of diet, so that the discovery added yet another string to his bow of murder.

Perhaps Klix was usurping a little, for his fondness of fishing ultimately nearly cost him his life. The next spate brought the salmon hosts from the sea, and they, too, fought their way up with the sun's setting to the gravel beds which for ages have seen the coming of the salmon harvest. So Klix one night again saw something moving idly in the dark waters. The moonlight glistened momentarily on a wet and shining body, and with a scream Klix stooped and struck. He stuck his claws deeply into the wet, firm flesh, and next moment he was dragged across the surface, feet foremost, a roar of angry waters on every side, rising, rising to engulf him.

For Klix had struck at a Silver King from the sea!

The effect was weird, startling, ghostly. A moment earlier the surface had been serene, with only the musical tinkle among the pebbles, and no living thing seemed to be astir in those icy, mirthless waters. Then Klix struck, and instantly the surface became alive, mammoth fish, hitherto lying like submerged logs, dashing pell-mell for the depths, churning the surface in phosphorescent foam, while crossed and criss-crossed the silver daggers flashed from bank to bank.

Klix, I say, had buried his claws deeply, and even if he could have withdrawn them the thought would not have occurred to him before he was carried under. What really saved him was one of those submerged posts, driven into the river bed by the bailiffs and bristling rusty nails to defy the nets of the poachers. This post had arrested an elm branch in its travels. The salmon passed under the branch, and Klix was caught in the arch and luckily torn away. He flapped heavily ashore, where for a while he sat preening his feathers and glowering angrily towards the dark waters, never again to make the same deadly error.

And yet another harvest night the brown owls knew. The leaves were drifting earthwards now, and truly the woods were a world of wasting ghosts. Three chicks had been successfully reared since Klix became independent, and the last had fared the best, because there were five to feed him. Five, I say, but in truth the parents, with their upgrown family, had become a trifle indolent, and the last chick was fed chiefly by his brothers and sisters. So, any night, what at first appeared to be a veritable flock of owls might have been seen assembled in one tree, or flying from tree to tree together, though in truth the flock numbered only six. But six owls go a long way in the darkness.

One night a stableman placed some sticks to dry on the little oven of the harness-room fire. Another stableman came in to warm his hands, and added more coals to the blaze. Then the first forgot the sticks, and the premises were left for the night. So the sticks caught light, and an hour later the whole rickety range was alight.

Some time later the owls were attracted by a great blaze in the valley, so they went down to see. The outbuilding of Klix's brief captive days was on fire, and right merrily it burnt. Soon the rickyard joined in the conflagration, while men and women ran and shouted, carrying buckets of water, which were as useless as drops of oil on a troubled sea.

The air was full of birds, some hurling themselves into the blaze, others, the more astute, flying from tree to tree in a panic of excited dread. Soon, however, the owls realized that the disturbance was no affair of theirs, so they settled down to profit by it while they could. And profit they did, for across the pasture land towards the gorse thickets of the hillside there moved a living train of rats and mice, which slew each other and were slain in the blind panic of their exit. And the brown owls pounced and rose and pounced, presently to be assisted by flotillas of their screeching and mewing relatives, which continued to hunt the gorse bushes till far on in the following day.

By the early winter Klix had acquired his full voice, and could now hoot in the most approved Shakespearian style. Hitherto he had contented himself with shrieking and hissing, but having now learnt to hoot he spent hours at it till the whole wood rang. And in truth there were many owls in the woods that early winter.

It proved a severe winter, and in spite of their soft, warm feathers the owls suffered as much as any of the wild birds about them. Where now the mice millions which once had swarmed in the grass? Deeper underground, and not to be seen. Where the fat trout which had glistened in the shallows? Hiding in the deepest and darkest pools till even Lutra the otter, and Quask, the sentinel heron, were hungry. Where the rat armies which had swarmed in the flood of moonlight between the man-made buildings? Safely under the floors of those same buildings. Even the small birds sought the most secure retreats with the fall of darkness, and Klix and his clan fell hungry.

His mother flew into an iron tank, half full of ice. I rather think she tried to settle on its icy rim, lost her footing, and fell. So weak was she that she could not make the vertical ascent from her prison, and beating herself against the walls she duly perished there. His father lived, and shared what food he got with his young, though he himself was starving. One of the young, the one next to Klix, flew into the face of a fox for some strange reason. Perhaps he

thought, in the grip of that hunger which knows no
fear, that he could kill the fox, but the fox killed
him. Another of the young attacked a hare one
brilliantly moonlight night, and somehow broke a
wing during the encounter, and ere the Frost King
sheathed his sword only Klix and his father sur-
vived. They remained together all winter, sleeping
side by side for mutual warmth, but when spring
came they parted, each with his native aims.

Strange that Klix should choose the blackened
ruins of the homestead outhouse as his nesting site,
yet thither that spring he led his bride, and in a
crevice of the offending chimney-flue she laid her
first white, oval egg. But the owner of the property
now knew too much about the ways of brown owls
to encourage their patronage. He loved to hear the
song birds in his groves, and he could sleep without
that mellow hooting from the elms. So the female
owl was shot on her way to her nest, but within
twenty-four hours Klix turned up with a second
wife, who at once took charge of the orphan egg,
and added another to it.

She, too, was shot within a week; yet a third mate
Klix produced, and she in turn took charge of the
nest and its contents, though the eggs were not of
her laying. Then the landlord decided that Klix
deserved to rear his young in peace. Thrice he had
ventured matrimony with its manifold joys and
risks, and doubtless he would have married again
and yet again till the supply of eligible ladies gave
out. But, after all, Klix himself was not much to
be admired, for evidently he chose marriage as the

simpler alternative to sitting the eggs himself. Still, he must have loved those eggs or he would have forsaken the place as manifestly perilous, and surely it demands ideals of the loftiest kind to love a colourless, nearly-round egg?

That season Klix and his mate reared eight sturdy young among the ruins of the building which had marked an epoch in his own life, but the following winter Klix himself met his fate in a strange and unusual way. The owner of the property had recently purchased a motor car, and motor cars were few in that quiet backwash of life. One night the car entered the avenue with its headlamps glaring, when something, descending from the trees, flew straight into one of the lamps with a force that cracked the glass. On the driver dismounting he found a dead owl in the centre of the way, while a short distance from it lay a little dark object which proved to be a bat!

So the exact facts will never be known. Had Klix been carrying the bat when, attracted by the dazzling light, he flew into the glass, or had the bat flown into the light, hotly and heedlessly pursued by Klix? Perhaps the latter, for to those who kill vengeance often comes by the feeblest and the smallest of their prey.

THE GREY SENTINEL

The woman who lived at the lodge had become quite accustomed to the grey heron which stood each morning at the river bend as she passed on her way for the milk, and the heron had become quite used to her. At first he would fly off as her footsteps drew near along the pathway above, but soon he came to know that she would not harm him. So she saw him every day, standing at the edge of the rapid water, sometimes with neck rigidly extended at an angle of forty-five degrees, motionless and ready to strike, sometimes stiff and erect, but always the embodiment of alert intentness. And never, never did she see him with his neck gracefully and reposefully curved as so many artists would have it.

One day, as the woman drew near, a strange jumble of noises, which might have been truly terrifying had it been dark, met her ears, and peering through the budding branches she saw the bird dancing about in ungainly hops, using his big wings, and striking apparently at the stones about his feet. She watched some seconds ere she could make out what was taking place, then in addition to the croakings and raspings of the bird, she distinguished an angry hissing and chattering, and knew that the heron was fighting some enemy. Presently she discovered something moving quickly among the stones, so quickly, indeed, that she could hardly get her gaze focused upon it, something she took to be a large, shaggy, and unusually dark-coloured squirrel. The bird was striking repeatedly at the animal, which at length darted into a cranny.

The heron was evidently very angry indeed, for he proceeded to march solemnly about, looking for his foe, when suddenly the animal leapt at him like a ray of light, bowling him clean over and dislodging a whole handful of feathers.

At that the heron made off, and the woman, realizing that she had seen something unusual, looked up the keeper on her way home and described the unknown beast. He was absolutely nonplussed, for the only animal which seemed in any way to tally with her description was the pine marten, and twenty years had passed since the last marten was heard of in that range.

Evidently Stilts, the heron, had received quite a bad shock, for the woman never again saw him at that corner. It was the early spring, but since Stilts was only a year old he had as yet no thoughts of matrimony. The heronry to which he belonged and in which he was born was in the heart of the beech wood within a mile of the bend, and so far he had confined himself chiefly to that locality. Now, however, with the call of the spring strongly upon him, it was by no means certain that the darkest hour before the dawn would find him back at the heronry.

For Stilts fished by night as well as by day, and whether he considered himself diurnal or nocturnal in habits I could never quite make out. It seemed to me that he slept when in the mood for nothing else, which was not very often, and certainly no man ever saw him sleeping. Having eaten his fill he would alight on the topmost twig of a certain high larch which stood alone and in solitary possession of the great pasture across the river from the heronry. Conspicuous from afar he would gaze anxiously about for fully five minutes after alighting, staring long and carefully in this direction and that before finally his head began to settle. Though so conspicuous, his choice of a resting place was a wise one, for nothing on earth could have taken him unawares at his lofty outlook in the midst of that little Sahara, and often he would spend many hours there, taking his repose. If he slept, it must have been with his eyes open, for should a pedestrian on the highroad nearly a mile away so much as climb the wall into the pasture, Stilts would raise his head instantly to inquire into the matter.

He was very much of a creature of regular ways and appointed places, and having forsaken the bend he took up his stance each morning at the edge of a sandy bay two miles farther down-stream, and though he had lost his distrust of the woman, he certainly trusted no one else. Alighting to fish, he would gaze all round as when he alighted to rest, and his fishing places, like his roosting places, were chosen with a view to complete immunity from surprise. He did not mind people watching him from the road, and he took no notice whatever of passing traffic, but he was for ever on the alert for suspicious signs which augured possible treachery.

As a matter of fact, Stilts was by no means easy

to discern among his watery surrounds, for his seemingly conspicuous grey coat had a wonderful way of blending with the grey shimmer on the water or the glancing lights of the rushes. When, indeed, one saw him with the water as a background, as for example, when one looked down the river from the bridge, he was invisible as any bird could be, for Stilts had a habit of keeping perfectly still. If really suspicious, he would stroll into the rushes, and stand, in their shelter with head up, his body hidden, his keen eyes peering above the sea of waving wands, and then, indeed, the keenest of eyes could never have picked him out. But in all the length and breadth of that valley there was none with eyes so keen as Stilts's.

Stilts did not trust the human anglers which vied with him for the spoils of the stream, but at the same time he knew that fishing rods and landing nets were quite harmless weapons so far as he was concerned. And the anglers obtained many peeps into his strange ways—indeed, the old man who had pensioned himself off to spend the remainder of his days fishing for perch in the loch, declared that he could set his watch by that grey post of a bird which alighted each morning at a certain point where the river flowed in.

"At five minutes to one he alights, at twelve minutes past two he goes, and I defy anyone to see him when there's a ripple on the surface to match the grey of his coat!" said the old angler.

Moreover, it seemed that Stilts knew the wild bird life about him at least as well as the man himself. Whether he had his own names for the squeaking coots and the ducking dabchicks we cannot, of course, know, but at any rate he knew that the family of buzzards which every day circled and soared high over the loch were not to be feared— even though they had the gliding, hovering flight of the eagle. Many a man might, indeed, have mistaken them for eagles, but Stilts knew. When first they arrived, he would regard them closely, shifting uneasily from leg to leg, but presently he would dismiss them from his thoughts and go on with his fishing.

Quite different was it, however, when one day a real eagle passed, for Stilts took one ungainly hop for the rushes, where he hid himself like a quail, while all around him the smaller birds stampeded madly for such cover as there was.

As a matter of fact, Stilts had good cause to watch the skies, for there still lived in his veins the evil memory of the falconry days when his kind, which now holds the lowly position of questionable vermin, was as sacred to man's possession as the pheasant is to-day.

One morning Stilts was calmly fishing when he heard a terrific swish of wings approaching behind him. A peregrine had stooped at him from the crest of the mountain ridge fully a mile away, sweeping down the steep face at a speed which literally dazzled the eye. For once Stilts was caught off his guard. There was no time to dive into the rushes, and it would have been of no use in any case. To outspeed the falcon was impossible, yet if he re-

STILTS TOOK ONE UNGAINLY HOP FOR THE RUSHES

mained where he was he would most assuredly be decapitated.

Harking back from his hunted ancestors, came the prompting to Stilts as to what to do. He rose, and made for the centre of the river, flying so low that his big wings " flap-flap-flapped " across the surface like those of a rising swan, and so up-stream, never leaving the surface. The falcon banked, swerved, and for the next mile he cut rings round the heron, rising constantly above, adjusting his speed, but fearing to stoop. For it is the way of the peregrine, and his only way, to strike down his quarry in a meteor plunge, and the heavier the quarry the greater must be the space below to exhaust the stoop. This peregrine could not strike because there was an insufficient depth of air below, and so up the river they went, across the stretch of blackgame swamp land, to the point at which the timber began.

Here there was a giant plane, its roots undermined by the river, forming a shadowy warren which the otters frequented when the salmon ran. Stilts made for that haven. It was contrary to his nature to hide himself in such a place, yet deep into one of the passageways he crowded, for with such a foe on his trail he would have sought fire.

The peregrine hung about for ten minutes or more, then he rocketed and switchbacked into the blue heights which were rightly his.

By now the gilt-edged daffodil harvest was fading from the burn banks; by now the grey hens were busy with their own affairs, and the red birds of the greater heights had their families. Stilts had nothing in particular to keep him there, and there were at least two reasons why he should leave. So he left, and for several months he lived a nomadic life. Not entirely nomadic, for he stuck to one great circle, dotted around which were certain familiar, beloved points. The mated birds, with their young, which he left behind, still stuck to their little routines and their regular coming and going, but Stilts became one of that vast number of summer herons which, since only a small percentage nest annually, spent the days of sunshine and cloud free to pursue their own affairs.

Stilts had grown up to inherit certain fishing rights in his own home country. No one had ever disputed his right to fish at the corner, at the bay, at the loch head; he had simply fallen into his place in the community to which he belonged. Now, however, he voyaged down the river, the sentinel stars overhead—past the light of many a homestead, flickering as figures passed the windows, past the glimmer of more than one star-lit loch, encircled more than one blue shoulder round which the river curled—over dark fir forests, emerald bracken beds, and skimming low beneath the scowl of overhanging crags, as was his wont—till he came at length to the broken wold country, dear to the hearts of all men, but most of all to the sturdy sons of Border blood.

It was the same old river, but how different here from the old Galloway Highlands—here where Stilts made his new home! Dawn found him hungry rather than tired. He had covered many miles, for he had followed unerringly the silver highway, and choosing a sheltered corner where a sluggish burn joined the river, he settled to fish. He had not been there very long, however, when another heron appeared, and began to circle round him, croaking angrily. Stilts struck at it several times, refusing to leave his stance, and presently the aggressive one flew off to the fir wood. It returned ten minutes later accompanied by six other herons, and speedily they drove him off, the centre of a turmoil of wrath. Several times during the succeeding days this kind of thing happened in a modified form, and so Stilts came to know the law, which later, when he himself became one of the " minds " of the community, he rigidly upheld. He learnt to establish his fishing rights with due regard for the rights of others, for with so many anglers and but one river, observance of this kind was necessary for the welfare of all. So, when Stilts left his early morning stance he knew that the patch of water would not be disturbed till he came back at the same hour next morning, and had others poached on it during his absence, neither they nor he would have done much good. This is the law, then, which all good fishers follow—observe each other's chosen beats.

But Stilts's new range was enormous, and embraced the tidal mouth of the river. Here a different order prevailed, or rather no order at all, for during the flood tide the herons came in like gulls, alighting anywhere to do their fishing. The brackish water was, indeed, common property, for the fish it bore were from the endless bounty of the sea, thousands to-day, none to-morrow, and no amount of over-fishing when the waters were heavy with fish spoilt to-morrow's chances.

Though fish formed the bulk of the heron's food, he was by no means averse to other fare. Anything alive which he could conveniently swallow he would readily gulp, and one day he swallowed a weasel which attacked him—not without a good deal of obstinacy on the part of the weasel. Not far from the river mouth was a patch of plough land, which that summer was subjected to a plague of mice, and regularly several long-legged herons were to be seen strolling about it, gulping mice as hard as they could get them down.

Stilts, I say, was now covering an immense area, and for all his wariness he visited at least once a week a certain stance in the centre of a large town. Within sixty yards on either side of him were rows of human dwellings, about the water walls of which children played. Motor horns hooted and the rumble of the mills filled the air, but here, where he knew man belonged, Stilts had no fear of him. It was a peculiar feature of this shy bird—he could do with man in his proper setting, but he was scared at the sight of him away from that setting. Stilts was, indeed, a strange mixture of fearlessness and timidity, but behind it all was a power of discrimination which showed him and his race to be high up on the scale of intelligence.

Stilts's wanderings consisted of a rough circle of perhaps a hundred miles in circumference. He might travel nine miles a day or ninety according to his mood, the weather, and the fishing. Dotted about on this great range he had his roosting places, as a trapper has his shelter cabins, and most of these roosting places were recognized by his kind and high up in the forest fastnesses. There, at daybreak or after the fall of dusk, the herons would alight, perhaps two or three of them, perhaps eight or nine. They never roosted singly, they never roosted anywhere save at these selected quarters, where the signs of their frequency were visible to the human eye. So, throughout their lives, herons, like kingfishers and otters, and indeed most who wring their livings from the waterways, recognize certain places as their own, and generation after generation they frequent those places. Thus the herons' roosting place may become their nesting place should the foresters fell the trees which previously they favoured.

But, when the herons gathered together to roost, it seemed that they met only to disagree, and in the darkness of the night eerie and strange were the sounds they uttered as they alighted—gaspings, gurglings, hissings, stranglings, such an assortment of noises that none who knew not the heron's vocabulary could have guessed what kind of creatures were astir. For twenty minutes or so they would keep this up, then, tired of disagreeing, they would settle to sleep, each bird on the topmost branch of the tree he or she had chosen.

As the autumn came on, Stilts sought again the land that he had loved, the land of his own people, his own city, but it is hard, on returning to one's native nook, to learn that one's places have been filled, one's corners usurped, that others have taken over that which once was undividedly one's own; hard to find oneself a stranger, and perhaps an un-invited stranger, amidst those settings which, throughout one's wanderings, have lived in the memory as Home—but that, indeed, was what Stilts found. It seemed at first that there was no room for him, here in his own land and among his own people, for when he alighted, as so many times before, on the old familiar fir, he was driven out by another heron, which now owned the place. He went back to the nest in which he was born, to be buffeted from the tree by two aggressive strangers —his own parents, had he but known it. The corner, the sandy bay, the loch head—each had been bagged by precocious upstarts, which sent him about his business. But he learnt, ere long, that there was indeed room for him, as there is room in every community for the stranger who will observe the old, old law, and is prepared to fit in with the working order as he finds it.

That winter Stilts, frequenting the heronry at regular intervals, returned one evening with a mate. Clearly she was a stranger in a strange land. One could tell that by the sit of her neck, but Stilts had by now re-established himself, and the other herons came at once to regard his bride as a natural part of the furnishings.

Stilts's parents had evidently decided not to trouble with family affairs that spring. Indeed, they com-pletely disappeared about mid-winter from the heronry—gone off touring, I suppose—and Stilts and his mate took possession of the gigantic pile of sticks on which he was born.

One day, several weeks later, when the dozen or so pairs of herons which that year were breeding in the heronry had their young, there was a tremendous hubbub in that part of the wood. So great was it, indeed, that all the herons which belonged to the place—and there must have been sixty of them, though only twenty-four were really concerned—came flooding back, to circle in the heavens high above, lending at least the strength of their voices to the general hubbub.

The keeper thought that some egg collectors must be raiding the place, so taking his dogs he went to see. By the time he reached the heronry the hubbub had subsided, and he could find nothing to account for it. He was about to give it up and go home when he noticed something lying under the trees directly beneath one of the largest nests. Near to it lay a young heron, evidently dragged from out the nest. It was severely mauled and quite dead, though muscular action was still going on.

As for the other thing—it, too, was dead. Its skull appeared to have been traversed, as though by a bayonet bill. The creature itself was a very beautiful creature, resembling a great, dark - coloured squirrel, save that its breast was of flaming orange. A tree weasel—yes, a pine marten, though twenty-one years had passed since the last was heard of on that range!